LICENSE TO GRILL

LICENSE TO GRILL

Copyright © 2025 by Cider Mill Press Book Publishers LLC.

This is an officially licensed book by Cider Mill Press Book Publishers LLC.

All rights reserved under the Pan-American and International Copyright Conventions.

No part of this book may be reproduced in whole or in part, scanned, photocopied, recorded, distributed in any printed or electronic form, or reproduced in any manner whatsoever, or by any information storage and retrieval system now known or hereafter invented, without express written permission of the publisher, except in the case of brief quotations in critical articles and reviews.

The scanning, uploading, and distribution of this book via the internet or via any other means without permission of the publisher is illegal and punishable by law. Please support authors' rights, and do not participate in or encourage piracy of copyrighted materials.

13-Digit ISBN: 9781400350667

10-Digit ISBN: 1400350662

This book may be ordered by mail from the publisher. Please include $5.99 for postage and handling. Please support your local bookseller first!

Books published by Cider Mill Press Book Publishers are available at special discounts for bulk purchases in the United States by corporations, institutions, and other organizations. For more information, please contact the publisher.

Cider Mill Press Book Publishers
"Where good books are ready for press"
501 Nelson Place
Nashville, Tennessee 37214
cidermillpress.com

Typography: Sofia Pro, Futura LT Pro Black

Image Credits: Pages 14, 32–33, 41, 42, 45, 53, 64–65, 71, 75, 82, 89, 104–105, 106, 109, 128–129, 134, 137, 142, 147, 150, 156–157, 160–161, 192, 197, and 204 courtesy of Cider Mill Press. All other images used under official license from Shutterstock.

Printed in Malaysia

24 25 26 27 28 PJM 5 4 3 2 1

First Edition

LICENSE TO GRILL

100 BBQ RECIPES FOR YOUR EYES ONLY

CIDER MILL PRESS

BOOK PUBLISHERS

INTRODUCTION 7

BEEF & LAMB 12

POULTRY & PORK 54

SEAFOOD 92

APPETIZERS, SIDES & SALADS 122

RUBS, MARINADES & SAUCES 172

APPENDIX 206

INDEX 219

INTRODUCTION

Compared to preparing a meal on the stove or in the oven, never mind a microwave or Crock-Pot, cooking over fire is hard work.

But it is also a form of luxury. For everything else becomes ancillary. A great meal prepared over fire is not something one can stumble into, improvise in the course of a busy day, or half pay attention to. It requires forethought, careful consideration, significant time, unflagging attention.

One must gather fuel, be it charcoal, propane, or wood. One must select ingredients that justify the effort necessary to build the fire. Once it is lit, one must stand by so that it reaches the ideal level of controlled chaos, neither goes out nor gets out of hand. When the food goes on, the real work begins: making sure the power of the fire does not ruin the food before the smoke can enhance it.

These parameters open spaces that are too often closed off. A search for kindling turns into a walk in the woods. The period waiting for charcoal to become coals is spent in silent contemplation. The warm glow of the fire invites others to approach, fostering connections and conversations typically off-limits.

And, once the cooking commences, one must become wholly alive, training each sense upon the grill. What is happening to the meat? What color is the smoke rising from it? What is the fire doing? What size and shape log does it need? How does the fire sound? Pay attention as you go to reposition that salmon fillet—has the hot spot shifted somewhere else? Cooking on the grill is an illuminating blend of science and art—a process of observing and interrogating what is happening before you, and then using the reflexes instilled by experience to fashion the correct response.

Consistency is everything in cooking, and fire is consistency's sworn enemy. It is unreliable, ever-changing. Capable of lashing out and ruining food in one instant, failing to supply enough heat in the very same spot in another.

Whatever end one envisions for an ingredient, fire is set on complicating that aim. If you are using wood and/or charcoal, hot and cool spots will shift every 10 minutes or so, forcing one to not just be focused on the food that has been placed on the grill, but what the temperature is in a certain spot compared to when you were there last. You cannot let the fire get too low, but you also need to make sure it does not get too hot, that the coal bed retains its level, that the grate is at the proper height. Sometimes, you need to remove every ember beneath a piece of meat, relying on time and ambient heat to get the interior where you want it. Then, for the very same piece of meat, a brief spell over blistering heat is required to get the browned crust that instantly signals "delicious."

Such volatility and variation are far from ideal cooking conditions, but they are incredibly energizing. You cannot grow complacent or disenchanted cooking over fire, you cannot rely on formulas or reputation, or make assumptions about what will happen. It might be less stressful to have such safety nets in place, but they are also the enemies of creativity, preventing one from paying attention to the present moment, and extinguishing the passion necessary to power through the endless repetitions that cooking entails. Grilling is a wonderful combination of ritual and mystery, where one follows the rote to get to a place where they know nothing. Like any worthwhile practice, it is mysterious and dynamic enough to fill each day with realizations, discoveries, and possibilities.

You will not be able to control it, but so long as you let the flame lead, you can dance with it.

To cook well on the grill, equally large measures of feel, expertise, and dedication are required. These can only be built over time, by standing through hundreds of barbecues, learning how to gauge the heat in each section with a quick pass of the hand, becoming able to judge an unseasoned log by its weight, understanding what the color of the smoke issuing from a piece of meat is telling you. Such a lengthy apprenticeship is possible to get through only with passion, but so long as you have that, and keep a few simple precepts in mind, you will manage.

People tend to equate fire with masculinity. Add meat into the equation and this macho conception gets pushed even further to the extreme, causing people to view grilling as a brief endeavor, where meat must be branded with the all-important sear before the potent flames can damage it completely. With this approach, standing by the grill becomes an anxious vigil, where the leader of a clan stands by, watching closely, hoping that they manage to intercede at precisely the right moment.

But this is misguided, for many reasons. Instead, the power of fire means you want to be gentle, to go slowly, to be patient, to keep some distance between the flames and the ingredients—particularly when cooking meat.

Meat, you'll recall, is a muscle.

Imagine, for a moment, that you are on an airplane. You've been cruising along smoothly for the past hour, eyes closed and headphones on.

Unexpectedly, the plane enters a pocket of turbulence, causing it to dip suddenly and shudder violently. After a few minutes, the plane gets through the rough patch and resumes making its way placidly toward the destination. But this rediscovered calm does not immediately translate to you. Without fail, entertaining the ultimate consequences of such turbulence will leave your body tense and rigid for a time.

That is what happens to meat when it is placed in a spot where either the flames or improperly high heat can get at it. As a tumultuous stretch 30,000 feet above sea level is an extreme environment for you, so is a ripping-hot grill for a piece of meat. It does not mind a bit of heat. But too much will send it into shock, contracting the muscle's fibers and removing all possibility of it attaining the tender, delicious result you envisioned when you brought it home.

To combat the inclination to strong-arm what goes on the grill, remember this: when grilling, you do not want the flames. Allowing them to make contact with what you're cooking will result in a charred exterior too acrid for anyone to enjoy, and an interior that is undercooked, unappetizing, and potentially harmful.

What you want is the smoke. The purpose of cooking over fire is not to exploit its tremendous power to make what was raw quickly edible, but to infuse whatever you are cooking with the sweet, earthy, and pleasantly bitter flavor of its spirit, the smoke.

We can hear you pleading: But what about the sear?

The sear: the brown, crusty exterior that is the first thing most think of when it comes to grilling.

We are not saying that the sear is not important.

We are saying that this too needs to be worked up to slowly. For the sear also makes the meat less vulnerable, preventing heat from getting at the interior with the same efficiency, and keeping the delicious smoke out. If it is granted too quickly, you are going to struggle to get the inside of the meat cooked through without that lovely exterior sliding from browned to burnt, from a crispy, delectable bit of contrasting texture to an unappealing casing. Light charring is fine, but if it goes beyond that, recook the steak.

This browning, known in the cooking world as the Maillard reaction, is the result of proteins and sugars reformulating as new compounds when exposed to heat, introducing new aromas and flavors to the proceedings. It is an essential part of enjoying meat, but even this miraculous transformation takes a back seat to what is conferred by the smoke.

As cooking on the grill is about controlling exposure to heat, you need to be able to gauge that heat. This is less of a concern on gas grills, where you have more control, but there will still be hot spots. For those who grill over charcoal, the heat issuing from the coals is not going to be uniform. It is going to be tepid in some spots and blistering in others, and identifying where these are, and which areas lie somewhere between, is essential. Generally, you can determine the heat in each section of the grill by placing your hand right above the grate.

Extremely high heat is present in any spot you cannot leave your hand over for even two seconds.

High heat will allow for the hand to remain for two seconds before you need to move it away.

Medium heat accommodates you for five seconds, and low dwells in a zone where your hand is OK for nine or more. Testing the grill to determine where these temperatures reside, and checking in on them frequently, will let you know where an ingredient should start—high for fish fillets and thinner cuts, low for thick pieces of meat, vegetables, and whole fish—and how to adjust if an ingredient communicates that it isn't in the right spot.

Touching the meat to determine whether it is properly cooked is another indispensable habit to develop. When you are a true pro, you will be able to tell what's going on inside simply by pressing down with your tongs. But before you have this feel, it's good to be hands on. A good, ahem, rule of thumb is to put each of your fingertips (one at a time) against the tip of your thumb, and use the index finger on your other hand to press against the pad below the thumb. The changes in how that pad feels for each finger will let you know what the various levels of doneness are for meat—the pinkie is well-done, the ring finger is medium-well, the middle finger is medium, and the index finger is what a medium-rare piece of meat should feel like.

It is also important to monitor the color of the smoke issuing from the food. So long as you see gray or blue smoke, you are OK. The second you see white smoke, transfer whatever you are grilling to a cooler spot on the grill, as that pale smoke indicates that it is starting to burn. It may already be too late, but if you act quickly, you should be able to salvage the meal.

The grate should be scraped clean with a wire brush before any meat is placed on it, as the carbonized remains from your last session will lend whatever you are cooking an unpleasant bitterness. During longer cooks, it's not a terrible idea to give it an occasional scrub between rounds, as fat can build up on the metal and encourage flare-ups. Though frequent grilling will season the grate (much like a cast-iron pan) and prevent food from sticking, for leaner cuts, it is perfectly fine to brush it with a bit of olive or canola oil.

These tips will not make you a master, but they will put you in position to avoid disaster, and sustain your enthusiasm. Do your best to keep them in mind, and reread this section often until they are ingrained.

Above all else, remember: your job when grilling is to care for the fire. Should the fire go out, all that time and energy will be for naught, all your grand plans dashed. Should the fire get out of control, your home, and your life, may be imperiled. You have been charged not only with cooking, but with caretaking. Act accordingly.

BEEF & LAMB

Chances are, you purchased this book primarily for the preparations in this chapter. And, considering that the addition of smoke makes the flavor of red meat absolutely perfect, it's an easy stance to understand.

YIELD: 2 SERVINGS / **TOTAL TIME:** 45 MINUTES

1 LB. NEW YORK STRIP STEAK

SALT, TO TASTE

1 TABLESPOON UNSALTED BUTTER

NEW YORK STRIP

1. Season the steak with salt and let it rest at room temperature.

2. Prepare a gas or charcoal grill, setting up one zone for direct heat and another for indirect.

3. Place your hand over the grate to test the heat in each section. Place the steak over medium heat—a spot you can leave your hand over for 5 seconds before you need to move it away. Cook until the steak is medium-rare (the interior is 130°F) and the exterior is nicely seared, 6 to 8 minutes, turning it over just once.

4. Remove the steak from the grill, place the butter on top, and let the steak rest for 2 minutes before serving.

YIELD: 2 SERVINGS / **TOTAL TIME:** 45 MINUTES

1 LB. RIB EYE

2 TEASPOONS KOSHER SALT

1 TABLESPOON UNSALTED BUTTER

RIB EYE

1. Season the steak with the salt and let it rest at room temperature.

2. Prepare a gas or charcoal grill, setting up one zone for direct heat and another for indirect.

3. Place your hand over the grate to test the heat in each section. Place the steak over high heat—a spot you can only leave your hand over for 2 seconds before you need to move it away. Cook until the steak is medium-rare (the interior is 130°F) and the exterior is nicely seared, 6 to 8 minutes, turning it over just once.

4. Remove the steak from the grill, place the butter on top, and let the steak rest for 2 minutes before serving.

YIELD: 2 SERVINGS / **TOTAL TIME:** 45 MINUTES

1 TABLESPOON CHIPOTLE CHILE POWDER

2 TEASPOONS KOSHER SALT

1 LB. T-BONE STEAK

2 TABLESPOONS EXTRA-VIRGIN OLIVE OIL

CHIPOTLE T-BONE

1. Place the chipotle powder and salt in a small bowl and stir to combine. Rub the steak with the olive oil and then coat it with the chipotle mixture. Let the steak rest at room temperature.

2. Prepare a gas or charcoal grill, setting up one zone for direct heat and another for indirect.

3. Place your hand over the grate to test the heat in each section. Place the steak over medium-high heat—a spot you can leave your hand over for 3 or 4 seconds before you need to move it away. Cook until the strip portion of the steak is medium-rare (the interior is 130°F) and the exterior is nicely seared, 6 to 8 minutes, turning it over just once.

4. Remove the steak from the grill and let it rest for 2 minutes before serving.

YIELD: 2 TO 4 SERVINGS / **TOTAL TIME:** 45 MINUTES

2 PORTERHOUSE STEAKS, EACH ABOUT 1½ INCHES THICK

2 TABLESPOONS EXTRA-VIRGIN OLIVE OIL

SALT AND PEPPER, TO TASTE

PORTERHOUSE

1. Rub the steaks with the olive oil, season them with salt, and let them rest at room temperature.

2. Prepare a gas or charcoal grill, setting up one zone for direct heat and another for indirect.

3. Place your hand over the grate to test the heat in each section. Place the steaks over medium-high heat—a spot you can leave your hand over for 3 to 4 seconds before you need to move it away. Cook until the strip portions of the steaks are medium-rare (the interiors are 130°F) and the exteriors are nicely seared, 6 to 8 minutes, making sure to turn the steaks over just once.

4. Remove the steaks from the grill, season them with pepper, and let them rest for 2 minutes before serving.

PORTERHOUSE
See page 19

YIELD: 2 SERVINGS / **TOTAL TIME:** 45 MINUTES

2 TABLESPOONS EXTRA-VIRGIN OLIVE OIL

1 TABLESPOON CHOPPED FRESH ROSEMARY

1 TEASPOON FRESH THYME

1 TO 1½ LB. FLANK STEAK

SALT AND PEPPER, TO TASTE

FLANK STEAK

1. Place the olive oil, rosemary, and thyme in a bowl and stir to combine. Rub the steak with the mixture, season it with salt, and let it sit at room temperature.

2. Prepare a gas or charcoal grill, setting up one zone for direct heat and another for indirect. Set up a grate over the coals.

3. Place your hand over the grate to test the heat in each section. Place the steak over medium-high heat—a spot you can leave your hand over for 3 or 4 seconds before you need to move it away. Cook until the steak

is medium-rare (the interior is 130°F), taking care not to overcook it, and the exterior is nicely seared, 6 to 8 minutes, turning it over just once.

4. Remove the steak from the grill, season it with pepper, and let it rest for 2 minutes before slicing it thin against the grain and serving.

YIELD: 2 SERVINGS / **TOTAL TIME:** 45 MINUTES

2 TABLESPOONS FINELY GROUND MEDIUM ROAST COFFEE

2 TEASPOONS KOSHER SALT

1 LB. TOP SIRLOIN

COFFEE-RUBBED SIRLOIN

1. Place the coffee and salt in a small bowl and stir to combine. Rub the steak with the mixture and let it rest at room temperature.

2. Prepare a gas or charcoal grill, setting up one zone for direct heat and another for indirect.

3. Place your hand over the grate to test the heat in each section. Place the steak over medium-high heat—a spot you can leave your hand over for 3 or 4 seconds before you need to move it away. Cook until the steak is medium-rare (the interior is 130°F) and the exterior is nicely seared, 6 to 8 minutes, turning it over just once.

4. Remove the steak from the grill and let it rest for 2 minutes before serving.

YIELD: 2 SERVINGS / **TOTAL TIME:** 1 HOUR

1 LB. FILET MIGNON

SALT, TO TASTE

1½ TABLESPOONS UNSALTED BUTTER

FILET MIGNON

1. Season the steaks with salt and let them sit at room temperature.

2. Prepare a gas or charcoal grill, setting up one zone for direct heat and another for indirect.

3. Place your hand over the grate to test the heat in each section. Place the steaks over medium heat—a spot you can leave your hand over for 5 seconds before you need to move it away. Cook until the steaks are medium-rare (the interiors are 130°F) and the exteriors are nicely seared, 12 to 14 minutes, turning them over just once.

4. Remove the steaks from heat, place a pat of the butter on top of each one, and let them rest for 2 minutes before serving.

YIELD: 2 TO 4 SERVINGS / **TOTAL TIME:** 1 HOUR

2 NEW YORK STRIP STEAKS, EACH ABOUT 1½ INCHES THICK

2 TABLESPOONS EXTRA-VIRGIN OLIVE OIL

SALT, TO TASTE

2 TABLESPOONS FRESHLY GROUND BLACK PEPPER

3 TABLESPOONS UNSALTED BUTTER

1 SHALLOT, MINCED

½ CUP COGNAC

½ CUP HEAVY CREAM

2 TABLESPOONS CHOPPED FRESH PARSLEY

STRIP STEAKS
WITH PEPPERCORN
CREAM SAUCE

1. Rub the steaks with the olive oil and season them with salt. Let them rest at room temperature.

2. Prepare a gas or charcoal grill, setting up one zone for direct heat and another for indirect.

3. Place your hand over the grate to test the heat in each section. Place the pepper in a small saucepan and place it over medium heat—a spot you can leave your hand over for 5 seconds before you need to move it away—and toast it for 1 minute. Add the butter and shallot and cook, stirring occasionally, until the shallot has softened, about 3 minutes.

4. Remove the pan from heat and add the Cognac. Place the pan back over medium heat and cook until the Cognac has reduced by half. Should the Cognac ignite while it is cooking, shake the pan and wait for the flames to die out.

5. Stir in the cream and cook until the sauce has slightly thickened, 2 to 3 minutes. Stir in the parsley, season the sauce with salt, and remove the pan from heat.

6. Place the steaks over medium-high heat—a spot you can leave your hand over for 3 or 4 seconds before you need to move it away. Cook until the steaks are medium-rare (the interior is 130°F) and the exteriors are nicely seared, 6 to 8 minutes. Remove the steaks from the grill and let them rest for 2 minutes.

7. Ladle the sauce over the steaks and enjoy.

YIELD: 2 SERVINGS / **TOTAL TIME:** 1 HOUR

1 LONDON BROIL STEAK, ¾ TO 1 INCH THICK

2 TABLESPOONS EXTRA-VIRGIN OLIVE OIL

CHILE RUB (SEE PAGE 180)

CHILE-RUBBED LONDON BROIL

1. Rub the steak with the olive oil, apply the Chile Rub, and let the steak rest at room temperature.

2. Prepare a gas or charcoal grill, setting up one zone for direct heat and another for indirect.

3. Place your hand over the grate to test the heat in each section. Place the steak over medium heat—a spot you can leave your hand over for 5 seconds before you need to move it away. Cook until the steak is medium-rare (the interior is 130°F) and the exterior is nicely seared, 6 to 8 minutes, turning it over just once.

4. Remove the steak from the grill and let it rest for 2 minutes before slicing and serving.

YIELD: 4 SERVINGS / **TOTAL TIME:** 45 MINUTES

1 LB. GROUND BEEF

1 TABLESPOON EPIS (SEE PAGE 193)

2 TABLESPOONS DICED BELL PEPPER

2 TABLESPOONS DICED ONION

1 TEASPOON ADOBO SEASONING

2 TEASPOONS GARLIC POWDER

1 TEASPOON BLACK PEPPER, PLUS MORE TO TASTE

SALT, TO TASTE

4 SLICES OF CHEDDAR CHEESE

2 TABLESPOONS UNSALTED BUTTER

4 HAMBURGER BUNS, SPLIT OPEN

SPICY MAYONNAISE (SEE PAGE 215)

8 SLICES OF BACON, COOKED

CREOLE SMASH BURGERS

1. Prepare a gas or charcoal grill, setting up one zone for direct heat and another for indirect.

2. Place the ground beef, Epis, bell pepper, onion, adobo seasoning, garlic powder, and black pepper in a mixing bowl, season with salt, and stir until well combined.

3. Divide the mixture into 4½ oz. portions, form them into balls, and set them aside.

4. Place your hand over the grate to test the heat in each section. Season the tops of the burgers with salt and pepper and place them over medium heat—a spot you can leave your hand over for 5 seconds before you need to move it away—seasoned side down.

5. Using a small cast-iron skillet or a burger press, smash the burgers flat. Season the tops of the burgers with salt and pepper as they cook. Cook until they are browned, 2 to 3 minutes.

6. Flip the burgers over and sear on the other side, 2 to 3 minutes. Top each burger with a slice of cheese. Cook until the burgers are cooked through and the cheese has melted, 3 to 5 minutes.

7. Remove the burgers from the grill, place them on a plate, and tent with aluminum foil to keep them warm.

8. Spread the butter on the cut sides of the buns. Place them over medium heat and toast until they are just browned, 1 to 2 minutes.

9. Spread the Spicy Mayonnaise over the toasted buns, assemble the burgers with the patties and bacon, and serve.

CREOLE SMASH BURGERS

See page 31

YIELD: 6 SERVINGS / **TOTAL TIME:** 12 HOURS

5 LB. CENTER-CUT BEEF BRISKET

2 TABLESPOONS EXTRA-VIRGIN OLIVE OIL

BRISKET RUB (SEE PAGE 176)

COLESLAW (SEE PAGE 210), FOR SERVING

BBQ BRISKET

1. Trim any fatty areas on the brisket so that the fat is within approximately ¼ inch of the meat, keeping in mind that it is better to leave too much fat than too little.

2. Rub the brisket with the olive oil and then generously apply the rub, making sure to knead it into the meat. Cover the brisket with plastic wrap and chill it in the refrigerator for 2 hours.

3. Prepare a gas or charcoal grill, setting up one zone for direct heat and another for indirect.

4. Place your hand over the grate to test the heat in each section. Place the brisket over low heat—a spot you can comfortably leave your hand over for 9 seconds. Cook until the brisket is very tender and the interior temperature is 190°F to 200°F.

5. Remove the brisket from heat and let it rest for 20 to 30 minutes before slicing and serving alongside the Coleslaw.

YIELD: 2 TO 4 SERVINGS / **TOTAL TIME:** 24 HOURS

2 LBS. TRI-TIP STEAK

RED WINE & HERB MARINADE (SEE PAGE 188)

CHIMICHURRI SAUCE (SEE PAGE 196), FOR SERVING

RED WINE & HERB
TRI-TIP STEAK

1. Place the steak in a baking dish and pour the marinade over it. Let the steak marinate in the refrigerator overnight.

2. Prepare a gas or charcoal grill, setting up one zone for direct heat and another for indirect. Remove the steak from the refrigerator and let it rest at room temperature.

3. Place your hand over the grate to test the heat in each section. Place the steak over medium heat—a spot you can leave your hand over for 5 seconds before you need to move it away. Cook until the steak is medium-rare (the interior is 130°F) and the exterior is nicely seared, 10 to 12 minutes.

4. Remove the steak from the grill and let it rest for 2 minutes before slicing it thin against the grain and serving with the Chimichurri Sauce.

LICENSE TO GRILL

36

YIELD: 6 TO 8 SERVINGS / **TOTAL TIME:** 4 HOURS

6-RIB PRIME RIB ROAST

3 TABLESPOONS EXTRA-VIRGIN OLIVE OIL

4 GARLIC CLOVES, MINCED

1 SMALL SHALLOT, MINCED

2 TABLESPOONS KOSHER SALT

2 TABLESPOONS BLACK PEPPER

3 BUNCHES OF FRESH THYME

3 BUNCHES OF FRESH ROSEMARY

PRIME RIB

1. Rub the prime rib with 1 tablespoon of olive oil and let it rest at room temperature for 30 minutes.

2. Place the garlic, shallot, and remaining olive oil in a bowl and stir to combine. Rub the prime rib with the mixture and let it rest at room temperature for another 30 minutes.

3. Prepare a gas or charcoal grill, setting up one zone for direct heat and another for indirect.

4. Season the prime rib generously with the salt and pepper. Take the thyme and rosemary and evenly distribute them between the ribs. Using kitchen twine, secure the bunches of herbs so that they will stay in place when you turn the prime rib while it is cooking.

5. Place your hand over the grate to test the heat in each section. Place the prime rib over medium-low heat—a spot you can leave your hand over for 6 or 7 seconds before you need to move it away. Sear the prime rib all over, about 15 minutes, turning it as necessary.

6. Turn the ribs toward the hottest part of the grill and cook the prime rib until it is charred all over and medium-rare (the interior is 125°F), about 2 hours, turning it as necessary.

7. Remove the prime rib from heat and let it rest for 10 minutes before slicing and serving.

TRI-TIP STEAK
See page 36

YIELD: 4 SERVINGS / **TOTAL TIME:** 45 MINUTES

1 LB. GROUND BEEF

1 TEASPOON KOSHER SALT

½ TEASPOON BLACK PEPPER

1 EGG WHITE

⅓ CUP BREAD CRUMBS

4 SLICES OF AMERICAN CHEESE

8 SLICES OF THICK-CUT BACON, COOKED

HAMBURGER BUNS, SPLIT OPEN, FOR SERVING

BACON CHEESEBURGERS

1. Prepare a gas or charcoal grill, setting up one zone for direct heat and another for indirect.

2. Place all of the ingredients, except for the cheese, bacon, and hamburger buns, in a mixing bowl and work the mixture until well combined. Divide the mixture into four equal parts and form each one into a 1-inch-thick patty.

3. Place your hand over the grate to test the heat in each section. Place the burgers over medium-high heat—a spot you can leave your hand over for 3 or 4 seconds before you need to move it away. Cook for 5 minutes.

4. Flip the burgers over and cook until they are just about cooked through, 4 to 5 minutes.

5. Top each burger with a slice of the cheese and cook until the cheese is melted and the burgers are completely cooked through, 1 to 2 minutes.

6. Remove the burgers from heat, top each one with some of the bacon, and serve on hamburger buns.

YIELD: 4 SERVINGS / **TOTAL TIME:** 45 MINUTES

1 LB. GROUND BEEF

1 TEASPOON KOSHER SALT

½ TEASPOON WHITE PEPPER

1 EGG WHITE

⅓ CUP BREAD CRUMBS

4 SLICES OF CHEDDAR CHEESE

⅓ CUP BBQ SAUCE

8 SLICES OF THICK-CUT BACON, COOKED

¼ CUP PICKLED JALAPEÑOS

HAMBURGER BUNS, SPLIT OPEN, FOR SERVING

BBQ BURGERS

1. Prepare a gas or charcoal grill, setting up one zone for direct heat and another for indirect.

2. Place the ground beef, salt, pepper, egg white, and bread crumbs in a mixing bowl and work the mixture until well combined. Divide the mixture into four equal parts and form each one into a 1-inch-thick patty.

3. Place your hand over the grate to test the heat in each section. Place the burgers over medium-high heat—a spot you can leave your hand over for 3 or 4 seconds before you need to move it away. Cook for 5 minutes.

4. Flip the burgers over and cook until they are just about cooked through, 4 to 5 minutes.

5. Top each burger with a slice of the cheese and cook until the cheese is melted and the burgers are completely cooked through, 1 to 2 minutes.

6. Remove the burgers from heat, top each one with some of the BBQ sauce, bacon, and jalapeños, and serve on hamburger buns.

YIELD: 4 SERVINGS / **TOTAL TIME:** 45 MINUTES

1½ LBS. GROUND BEEF

1 ONION, GRATED

1 TEASPOON CHOPPED FRESH ROSEMARY

3 GARLIC CLOVES, MINCED

1 TEASPOON CUMIN

½ TEASPOON DRIED THYME

SALT AND PEPPER, TO TASTE

BEEF KEBABS

1. Prepare a gas or charcoal grill, setting up one zone for direct heat and another for indirect.

2. Place all of the ingredients in a mixing bowl and work the mixture with your hands until well combined. Form the meat into an oblong shape around 8 to 12 skewers and chill them in the refrigerator for 30 minutes.

3. Place your hand over the grate to test the heat in each section. Place the kebabs over medium heat—a spot you can leave your hand over for 5 seconds before you need to move it away. Grill the kebabs until they are charred all over and cooked through, 10 to 12 minutes, turning them as little as necessary.

4. Remove the kebabs from heat and let them rest for 2 minutes before serving.

YIELD: 4 TO 6 SERVINGS / **TOTAL TIME:** 3 HOURS

1 JALAPEÑO CHILE PEPPER, STEMMED, SEEDED, AND MINCED

3 GARLIC CLOVES, MINCED

½ CUP CHOPPED FRESH CILANTRO

¼ CUP AVOCADO OIL

JUICE OF 1 ORANGE

2 TABLESPOONS APPLE CIDER VINEGAR

2 TEASPOONS CAYENNE PEPPER

1 TEASPOON ANCHO CHILE POWDER

1 TEASPOON GARLIC POWDER

1 TEASPOON PAPRIKA

1 TEASPOON KOSHER SALT

1 TEASPOON CUMIN

1 TEASPOON DRIED OREGANO

¼ TEASPOON BLACK PEPPER

2 LBS. FLANK STEAK, TRIMMED

CARNE ASADA

1. Place all of the ingredients, except for the steak, in a large resealable plastic bag and stir to combine. Add the steak, place the bag in the refrigerator, and let the steak marinate for 2 hours.

2. Prepare a gas or charcoal grill, setting up one zone for direct heat and another for indirect.

3. Remove the steak from the marinade, pat it dry, and let it rest at room temperature.

4. Place your hand over the grate to test the heat in each section. Place the steak over medium-high heat—a spot you can leave your hand over for 3 or 4 seconds before you need to move it away. Grill until the steak is medium-rare (the interior is 130°F) and the exterior is nicely seared, 6 to 8 minutes, turning it over just once.

5. Remove the steak from heat and let it rest for 2 minutes before slicing it thin against the grain and serving.

YIELD: 4 TO 6 SERVINGS / **TOTAL TIME:** 2 HOURS

6 TABLESPOONS EXTRA-VIRGIN OLIVE OIL

3 TABLESPOONS RED WINE VINEGAR

JUICE OF 2 LEMONS

2 TEASPOONS CINNAMON

2 TABLESPOONS CORIANDER

1 TABLESPOON BLACK PEPPER

1 TEASPOON CARDAMOM

1 TEASPOON GROUND CLOVES

½ TEASPOON MACE

⅛ TEASPOON FRESHLY GRATED NUTMEG

1 TABLESPOON GARLIC POWDER

3 LBS. TOP SIRLOIN

2 YELLOW ONIONS, SLICED INTO THIN HALF-MOONS

SALT, TO TASTE

1 TEASPOON SUMAC

1 CUP FULL-FAT GREEK YOGURT, FOR SERVING

PITA BREAD (SEE PAGE 209), FOR SERVING

2 PERSIAN CUCUMBERS, DICED, FOR SERVING

2 ROMA TOMATOES, DICED, FOR SERVING

½ CUP FRESH MINT OR PARSLEY, TORN, FOR SERVING

BEEF SHAWARMA

1. Place the olive oil, vinegar, lemon juice, cinnamon, coriander, pepper, cardamom, cloves, mace, nutmeg, and garlic powder in a mixing bowl and stir to combine. Place the steak in a baking dish, pour the marinade over it, and place it in the refrigerator. Let the steak marinate for 1 hour.

2. Place the sliced onions in a baking dish and cover them with water. Add a pinch of salt and several ice cubes. Place the onions in the refrigerator and chill for 30 minutes.

3. Prepare a gas or charcoal grill, setting up one zone for direct heat and another for indirect.

4. Remove the steak and onions from the refrigerator. Let the meat sit at room temperature. Drain the onions, squeeze them to remove any excess water, and place them in a bowl. Add the sumac and toss to coat. Set the onions aside.

5. Place your hand over the grate to test the heat in each section. Place the steak over medium-high heat—a spot you can leave your hand over for 3 or 4 seconds before you need to move it away. Cook until the steak is medium-rare (the interior is 130°F) and the exterior is nicely seared, 8 to 10 minutes.

6. Remove the steak from heat and let it rest for 2 minutes before slicing it thin against the grain. To serve, place a dollop of yogurt on a pita and top with some of the meat, onions, cucumbers, tomatoes, and mint or parsley.

YIELD: 4 SERVINGS / **TOTAL TIME:** 1 HOUR

4 BONE-IN LAMB CHOPS, EACH ABOUT 1 INCH THICK

2 TABLESPOONS EXTRA-VIRGIN OLIVE OIL

KASHMIRI CHILE RUB (SEE PAGE 180)

RAITA (SEE PAGE 207), FOR SERVING

SPICY LAMB CHOPS WITH RAITA

1. Rub the lamb chops with the olive oil and then generously apply the rub, making sure both sides are coated. Let the lamb chops rest at room temperature.

2. Prepare a gas or charcoal grill, setting up one zone for direct heat and another for indirect.

3. Place your hand over the grate to test the heat in each section. Place the lamb chops over medium-low heat—a spot you can leave your hand over for 6 or 7 seconds before you need to move it away. Cook until the lamb

chops are medium-rare (the interior is 125°F) and the exteriors are nicely seared, 17 to 20 minutes, turning them over just once.

4. Remove the lamb chops from heat and let them rest for 3 minutes before serving with the Raita.

YIELD: 6 SERVINGS / **TOTAL TIME:** 24 HOURS

¾ CUP EXTRA-VIRGIN OLIVE OIL

¼ CUP FRESH ROSEMARY, CHOPPED

JUICE OF 3 LEMONS

4 GARLIC CLOVES, MINCED

4 LB. BONELESS LEG OF LAMB, BUTTERFLIED

SALT AND PEPPER, TO TASTE

ROSEMARY & LEMON LEG OF LAMB

1. Place the olive oil, rosemary, lemon juice, and garlic in a mixing bowl and mix thoroughly.

2. Season the lamb generously with salt and pepper and place it in a roasting pan. Pour the marinade over the lamb and let it marinate in the refrigerator overnight.

3. Prepare a gas or charcoal grill, setting up one zone for direct heat and another for indirect.

4. Remove the lamb from the refrigerator and let it rest at room temperature.

5. Place your hand over the grate to test the heat in each section. Place the lamb over medium heat—a spot you can leave your hand over for 5 seconds before you need to move it away. Cook until the lamb is medium-rare (the interior is 125°F) and the exterior is nicely seared, 30 to 35 minutes, turning it over just once.

6. Remove the lamb from heat and let it rest for 5 minutes before slicing and serving.

YIELD: 6 SERVINGS / **TOTAL TIME:** 3 HOURS AND 30 MINUTES

2½ LB. LAMB TENDERLOIN, TRIMMED

LAMB MARINADE (SEE PAGE 188)

CHIMICHURRI SAUCE (SEE PAGE 196), FOR SERVING

GRILLED LAMB LOIN
WITH CHIMICHURRI

1. Rub the lamb with the marinade and marinate it in the refrigerator for at least 2 hours.

2. Prepare a gas or charcoal grill, setting up one zone for direct heat and another for indirect.

3. Place your hand over the grate to test the heat in each section. Place the lamb over medium-high heat—a spot you can leave your hand over for 3 or 4 seconds before you need to move it away. Cook until the interior of the lamb is 140°F on an instant-read thermometer and the exterior is nicely seared, 15 to 20 minutes, turning it as little as possible.

4. Remove the lamb from the grill and let it rest for 10 minutes before slicing and serving with the Chimichurri Sauce.

YIELD: 4 SERVINGS / **TOTAL TIME:** 1 HOUR

1½ LBS. GROUND LAMB

1 ONION, GRATED

1 TEASPOON CHOPPED FRESH ROSEMARY

3 GARLIC CLOVES, MINCED

1 TEASPOON CUMIN

½ TEASPOON DRIED THYME

SALT AND PEPPER, TO TASTE

NAAN, FOR SERVING

FULL-FAT GREEK YOGURT, FOR SERVING

LAMB KEBABS

1. Prepare a gas or charcoal grill, setting up one zone for direct heat and another for indirect.

2. Place all of the ingredients, except for the naan and yogurt, in a mixing bowl and work the mixture with your hands until well combined. Form the meat into an oblong shape around 8 to 12 skewers and chill them in the refrigerator for 30 minutes.

3. Place your hand over the grate to test the heat in each section. Place the kebabs over medium heat—a spot you can leave your hand over for 5 seconds before you need to move it away. Grill the kebabs until they are charred all over and cooked through, 10 to 12 minutes, turning them as little as necessary.

4. Remove the kebabs from heat and let them rest for 2 minutes before serving with naan and yogurt.

LICENSE TO GRILL

POULTRY & PORK

Chicken, though lighter than beef and lamb, becomes no less exceptional over the flame. And pork, which is always obliging to a low-and-slow approach, supplies invaluable instruction and unmatched comfort in each and every preparation.

YIELD: 4 SERVINGS / **TOTAL TIME:** 24 HOURS

2 LBS. BONE-IN, SKIN-ON CHICKEN LEGS

PERI-PERI MARINADE (SEE PAGE 190)

LIME WEDGES, FOR SERVING

PERI-PERI CHICKEN

1. Place the chicken in a baking dish and rub it with half of the marinade. Let the chicken marinate in the refrigerator overnight. Store the remaining marinade in the refrigerator.

2. Prepare a gas or charcoal grill, setting up one zone for direct heat and another for indirect.

3. Remove the chicken from the marinade. Place your hand over the grate to test the heat in each section. Place the chicken over medium heat—a spot you can leave your hand over for 5 seconds before you need to move it away. Cook until the interior of the chicken is 165°F and the skin is nice and crispy, 25 to 30 minutes, turning it as little as possible.

4. Remove the chicken from heat and brush it with the remaining marinade. Serve with lime wedges and enjoy.

YIELD: 4 SERVINGS / **TOTAL TIME:** 24 HOURS

8 BONE-IN, SKIN-ON CHICKEN THIGHS

JERK MARINADE (SEE PAGE 187)

PICKLED GRILLED PINEAPPLE (SEE PAGE 126), FOR SERVING

JAMAICAN JERK CHICKEN

1. Place the chicken in a baking dish and pour the marinade over it. Let the chicken marinate in the refrigerator overnight.

2. Prepare a gas or charcoal grill, setting up one zone for direct heat and another for indirect.

3. Remove the chicken from the marinade and let it rest at room temperature.

4. Place your hand over the grate to test the heat in each section. Place the chicken, skin side down, over medium heat—a spot you can leave your hand over for 5 seconds before you need to move it away. Cook until the interior of the chicken is 165°F and the skin is nice and crispy, 20 to 25 minutes, turning it over just once.

5. Remove the chicken from the grill and let it rest for 2 minutes before serving with the Pickled Grilled Pineapple.

YIELD: 4 SERVINGS / **TOTAL TIME:** 4 HOURS AND 30 MINUTES

1 LB. PORK JOWL, CUT INTO ½-INCH-THICK SLICES

4 TEASPOONS LIGHT SOY SAUCE

2 TABLESPOONS DARK SOY SAUCE

1 TABLESPOON BROWN SUGAR

1 TEASPOON FINE SEA SALT

FRESH CILANTRO, CHOPPED, TO TASTE

3 DRIED CHILES DE ÁRBOL

SALSA MACHA (SEE PAGE 205), FOR SERVING

PORK TORO
WITH SALSA MACHA

1. Place all of the ingredients, except for the Salsa Macha, in a mixing bowl and stir until the pork jowl is coated. Place the bowl in the refrigerator and let the pork jowl marinate for 4 hours.

2. Prepare a gas or charcoal grill, setting up one zone for direct heat and another for indirect. Remove the pork jowl from the refrigerator and let it rest at room temperature for about 15 minutes.

3. Place your hand over the grate to test the heat in each section. Place the pork jowl over medium-high heat—a spot you can leave your hand over for 3 to 4 seconds before you need to move it away. Cook until the interior is 145°F and the exterior is crispy, 10 to 12 minutes, making sure to turn the pork jowl over just once.

4. Remove the pork jowl from the grill and let it rest for 5 minutes before serving with the Salsa Macha.

JAMAICAN JERK CHICKEN
See page 58

YIELD: 4 SERVINGS / **TOTAL TIME:** 24 HOURS

SALT, AS NEEDED

1 LB. PORK TENDERLOIN

2 PEACHES, PITTED AND QUARTERED

¼ CUP HONEY

2 CUPS MOLE MANCHAMANTELES (SEE PAGE 191), WARM

CORN TORTILLAS (SEE PAGE 208), WARM, FOR SERVING

LOMO Y MANCHAMANTELES

1. Fill a large saucepan with cold water and add 1¾ oz. of salt for every liter of water. Place the pork in the brine and let it sit in the refrigerator for 24 hours.

2. Prepare a gas or charcoal grill, setting up one zone for direct heat and another for indirect. Remove the pork from the brine, pat it dry, and let it rest at room temperature.

3. Place your hand over the grate to test the heat in each section. Place the pork over medium heat—a spot you can leave your hand over for 5 seconds before you need to move it away. Cook until the interior is 145°F and the exterior is seared, 10 to 12 minutes, turning it as necessary.

4. Remove the pork from the grill and let it rest for 5 minutes before slicing.

5. Brush the cut sides of the peaches with the honey and season them with salt. Place them on the grill over medium heat and cook until they are deeply charred, but not falling apart, about 6 minutes.

6. Spread ½ cup of the mole on each plate, top with slices of pork and the grilled peaches, and serve with tortillas.

LICENSE TO GRILL

YIELD: 6 TO 8 SERVINGS / **TOTAL TIME:** 2 HOURS

7 OZ. GUAJILLO CHILE PEPPERS, STEMMED AND SEEDED

1 TEASPOON CUMIN SEEDS

1 TEASPOON CORIANDER SEEDS

1 BAY LEAF

2 TABLESPOONS EXTRA-VIRGIN OLIVE OIL, PLUS MORE AS NEEDED

4 GARLIC CLOVES, MINCED

10 DRIED CHILES DE ÁRBOL, STEMMED AND SEEDED

7 TABLESPOONS APPLE CIDER VINEGAR OR CHAMPAGNE VINEGAR

SALT, TO TASTE

2 LBS. PORK TENDERLOIN, SLICED AND POUNDED ¼ INCH THICK

CORN TORTILLAS (SEE PAGE 208), WARM, FOR SERVING

LIME WEDGES, FOR SERVING

CECINA DE CERDO

1. Place the guajillo peppers in a dry skillet and toast over medium heat until they darken and become fragrant and pliable. Submerge them in a bowl of hot water and let them soak for 30 minutes.

2. Place the cumin and coriander seeds and bay leaf in the skillet and toast until they are fragrant, shaking the pan frequently. Grind the mixture into a powder using a mortar and pestle or a spice grinder.

3. Place the olive oil in a Dutch oven and warm it over medium heat. Add the garlic, cook until it is fragrant, and then add the chiles de árbol. Fry for 30 seconds and then remove the pan from heat.

4. Drain the guajillo peppers and reserve the soaking liquid. Place the guajillo peppers, spice powder, and garlic mixture in a blender and puree until smooth, adding the vinegar and soaking liquid as needed to attain a smooth and thick consistency. Season the puree with salt.

5. Place the pork tenderloin in a baking dish and pour the puree over it. Stir until coated and let it marinate in the refrigerator for at least 30 minutes. If time allows, marinate the pork for up to 24 hours.

6. Prepare a gas or charcoal grill, setting up one zone for direct heat and another for indirect. Lightly brush the grate with olive oil.

7. Place your hand over the grate to test the heat in each section. Place the pork over medium heat—a spot you can leave your hand over for 5 seconds before you need to move it away. Cook until the interior is 145°F and the exterior is seared, 10 to 12 minutes, turning it as necessary.

8. Remove the pork from the grill and let it rest for 2 minutes. Serve with tortillas and lime wedges.

POULTRY & PORK

CECINA DE CERDO

See page 63

YIELD: 8 SERVINGS / **TOTAL TIME:** 24 HOURS

½ TEASPOON ALLSPICE BERRIES

½ TEASPOON WHOLE CLOVES

3½ OZ. BLACK PEPPERCORNS

1 CINNAMON STICK

1 TEASPOON DRIED MEXICAN OREGANO

1 TEASPOON DRIED MARJORAM

8 GARLIC CLOVES

14 TABLESPOONS WHITE VINEGAR

SALT, TO TASTE

7 TO 8 LB. WHOLE TURKEY

4 ANAHEIM CHILE PEPPERS

1 HEAD OF GARLIC, HALVED AT ITS EQUATOR

3 BAY LEAVES

ESCABECHE (SEE PAGE 213)

LIME WEDGES, FOR SERVING

PAVO EN ESCABECHE

1. Place the allspice berries, cloves, peppercorns, and cinnamon stick in a dry skillet and toast until fragrant, shaking the pan frequently. Grind the mixture into a fine powder with a mortar and pestle or spice grinder.

2. Place the toasted spice powder, oregano, marjoram, garlic cloves, and three-quarters of the white vinegar in a blender and puree until the mixture is a thick paste. Add the remaining vinegar as needed to get the desired consistency. Season the paste with salt.

3. Coat the turkey with the recado blanco paste and let it marinate in the refrigerator overnight. If you do not have that much time, let it marinate for at least 2 hours.

4. Prepare a gas or charcoal grill, setting up one zone for direct heat and another for indirect.

5. Place your hand over the grate to test the heat in each section. Season the turkey with salt and place it over medium heat—a spot you can leave your hand over for 5 seconds before you need to move it away. Cook until it is deeply charred all over, but not cooked all the way through. Take care not to move the turkey too much on the grill so that the skin stays intact. Remove the turkey from the grill and set it aside.

6. Place the chiles on the grill over medium heat and cook, turning occasionally, until they are blistered and charred all over. Place them in a heatproof mixing bowl, cover it with plastic wrap, and let the chiles steam for 5 to 10 minutes. When they are cool enough to handle, remove the skin from the chiles, cut the chiles into strips, and set them aside.

7. Place the turkey in a stockpot or a saucepan that is deep enough to allow it to be covered with water by 2 to 3 inches. Add the head of garlic, bay leaves, and ½ cup of the recado blanco paste. Cover the turkey with water and bring to a simmer. Cook until the turkey is cooked through and just beginning to fall apart.

8. Add the Escabeche to the stew and season it with salt. Simmer for an additional 10 minutes.

9. Serve the turkey in large bowls, either on or off the bone, with good amounts of the Escabeche, lime wedges, and the strips of roasted chiles.

YIELD: 4 TO 6 SERVINGS / **TOTAL TIME:** 2 HOURS AND 30 MINUTES

2 TABLESPOONS PAPRIKA

1 TEASPOON TURMERIC

1 TEASPOON ONION POWDER

1 TEASPOON GARLIC POWDER

1 TABLESPOON DRIED OREGANO

¼ CUP EXTRA-VIRGIN OLIVE OIL

2 TABLESPOONS WHITE WINE VINEGAR

1 CUP FULL-FAT GREEK YOGURT

1 TEASPOON KOSHER SALT, PLUS MORE TO TASTE

2 LBS. BONELESS, SKINLESS CHICKEN THIGHS, CUBED

BLACK PEPPER, TO TASTE

LEMON WEDGES, FOR SERVING

CHICKEN KEBABS

1. Place the paprika, turmeric, onion powder, garlic powder, oregano, olive oil, vinegar, yogurt, and salt in a large bowl and whisk to combine.

2. Add the chicken and stir until it is coated. Let the chicken marinate in the refrigerator for 2 hours.

3. Prepare a gas or charcoal grill, setting up one zone for direct heat and another for indirect.

4. Remove the chicken from the marinade, thread it onto skewers, and season it with salt and pepper.

5. Place your hand over the grate to test the heat in each section. Place the skewers over medium heat—a spot you can leave your hand over for 5 seconds before you need to move it away. Grill until the chicken is cooked through and charred, about 15 minutes, turning the kebabs as little as possible.

6. Remove the skewers from heat, let them rest for 2 minutes, and serve with lemon wedges.

CHICKEN KEBABS
See page 67

YIELD: 10 SERVINGS / **TOTAL TIME:** 5 HOURS AND 30 MINUTES

5 LBS. PORK RIBS

½ CUP KOSHER SALT

2 TABLESPOONS LIGHT BROWN SUGAR

2 TABLESPOONS GARLIC POWDER

1 TABLESPOON ONION POWDER

1 TABLESPOON CHILI POWDER

1 TABLESPOON PAPRIKA

1 TABLESPOON CUMIN

MOLASSES BBQ SAUCE (SEE PAGE 201)

SLOW-COOKED MOLASSES BBQ RIBS

1. If your butcher has not already done so, remove the thin membrane from the back of each rack of ribs. Place the ribs in a roasting pan. Place all of the remaining ingredients, except for the Molasses BBQ Sauce, in a bowl and stir until combined. Rub the mixture in the bowl all over the ribs, making sure every inch is covered. Place the ribs in the refrigerator for 1 hour.

2. Prepare a gas or charcoal grill, setting up one zone for direct heat and another for indirect.

3. Place 2 to 3 layers of heavy-duty aluminum foil down, place the ribs on the foil, and securely wrap the ribs, making sure there are no holes or tears in the foil. Crimp the edges of the packet to seal.

4. Place your hand over the grate to test the heat in each section. Place the ribs over low heat—a spot you can comfortably leave your hand over for 9 seconds. Cook until the ribs begin to pull away from the bones, 3 to 4 hours, brushing them with some of the BBQ sauce every 20 or 30 minutes.

5. Remove the ribs from the foil packet and place them over medium-high heat—a spot you can leave your hand over for 3 or 4 seconds before you need to move it away. Cook the ribs until they have caramelized.

6. Remove the ribs from heat and let them rest for 20 minutes before serving.

LICENSE TO GRILL

YIELD: 4 SERVINGS / **TOTAL TIME:** 1 HOUR AND 30 MINUTES

2 RACKS OF BABY BACK PORK RIBS

2 CUPS BROWN SUGAR

2 TABLESPOONS KOSHER SALT

2 TABLESPOONS FRESHLY GROUND BLACK PEPPER

2 TABLESPOONS ANCHO CHILE POWDER (OPTIONAL)

1 LB. BACON FAT, CHILLED OR AT ROOM TEMPERATURE

BBQ SAUCE, FOR SERVING

BROWN SUGAR RIBS

1. Prepare a gas or charcoal grill, setting up one zone for direct heat and another for indirect.

2. If your butcher has not already done so, remove the thin membrane from the back of each rack of ribs.

3. Place the brown sugar, salt, pepper, and chile powder (if using) in a bowl and stir to combine. Generously rub the mixture over the ribs, and then coat the ribs with the bacon fat. Place 2 to 3 layers of heavy-duty aluminum foil down, place the racks of ribs, side by side, on top of the foil, and securely wrap the ribs, making sure there are no holes or tears in the foil. Crimp the edges of the packet to seal.

4. Place your hand over the grate to test the heat in each section. Place the ribs over medium heat—a spot you can leave your hand over for 5 seconds before you need to move it away. Cook until the ribs begin to pull away from the bones, 45 minutes to 1 hour.

5. Remove the ribs from the foil packet and place them over medium-high heat—a spot you can leave your hand over for 3 or 4 seconds before you need to move it away. Cook the ribs until they are lightly charred on each side.

6. Remove the ribs from the grill and serve with your favorite BBQ sauce.

YIELD: 4 SERVINGS / **TOTAL TIME:** 24 HOURS

8 CUPS WATER

¼ CUP KOSHER SALT

4 SEMIBONELESS QUAIL

1 TABLESPOON ALLSPICE BERRIES

1 CINNAMON STICK

3 TABLESPOONS CORIANDER SEEDS

2 TABLESPOONS CUMIN SEEDS

½ TEASPOON WHOLE CLOVES

2 TABLESPOONS BLACK PEPPERCORNS

1½ TEASPOONS WHITE PEPPERCORNS

3 BAY LEAVES

1 TEASPOON DRIED OREGANO

1 TEASPOON DRIED MARJORAM

1 TABLESPOON ANCHO CHILE POWDER

3½ TABLESPOONS ORANGE JUICE

3½ TABLESPOONS FRESH LIME JUICE

2 TABLESPOONS EXTRA-VIRGIN OLIVE OIL

LIME WEDGES, FOR SERVING

CORN TORTILLAS (SEE PAGE 208), WARM, FOR SERVING

SALSA, FOR SERVING

GRILLED QUAIL

1. Place the water and salt in a saucepan and warm over low heat, stirring until the salt has dissolved. Remove the pan from heat and let the brine cool completely. Place the quail in the brine and let them sit in the refrigerator for 12 to 24 hours.

2. Remove the quail from the brine and let them air-dry in the refrigerator for 1 to 2 hours.

3. Place the allspice berries, cinnamon stick, coriander seeds, cumin seeds, cloves, peppercorns, and bay leaves in a dry skillet and toast until fragrant, shaking the pan frequently so that they do not burn. Grind the mixture into a fine powder with a mortar and pestle or spice grinder.

4. Place the toasted spice powder, oregano, marjoram, ancho chile powder, orange juice,

and lime juice in a blender and puree until the mixture is a smooth paste. Rub the paste over the quail and let them marinate in the refrigerator for at least 30 minutes.

5. Prepare a gas or charcoal grill, setting up one zone for direct heat and another for indirect. Lightly brush the grate with the olive oil.

6. Place your hand over the grate to test the heat in each section. Place the quail over medium-high heat—a spot you can leave your hand over for 3 to 4 seconds before you need to move it away—breast side down. Cook until they are crispy and caramelized, 2 to 3 minutes. Turn them over and cook until the interior is 140°F, 1 to 2 minutes.

7. Remove the quail from the grill and let them rest for 10 minutes before serving with lime wedges, tortillas, and salsa.

LICENSE TO GRILL

YIELD: 4 SERVINGS / **TOTAL TIME:** 45 MINUTES

1 LB. GROUND CHICKEN

½ TEASPOON WHITE PEPPER

1 EGG WHITE

1 TABLESPOON TERIYAKI SAUCE

4 PINEAPPLE RINGS, EACH ABOUT ½ INCH THICK

HAMBURGER BUNS, SPLIT OPEN, FOR SERVING

CHICKEN TERIYAKI BURGERS

1. Prepare a gas or charcoal grill, setting up one zone for direct heat and another for indirect.

2. Place all of the ingredients, except for the pineapple and hamburger buns, in a mixing bowl and work the mixture until well combined. Divide the mixture into four equal parts and form each one into a 1-inch-thick patty.

3. Place your hand over the grate to test the heat in each section. Place the burgers over medium-high heat—a spot you can leave your hand over for 3 or 4 seconds before you need to move it away. Cook for 5 minutes.

4. Place the pineapple over medium-high heat and cook until it is charred on both sides, about 5 minutes.

5. Flip the burgers over and cook until they are cooked through, 5 to 6 minutes.

6. Remove the pineapple and burgers from heat, top the burgers with the charred pineapple, and serve with hamburger buns.

LICENSE TO GRILL

YIELD: 4 SERVINGS / **TOTAL TIME:** 2 HOURS AND 30 MINUTES

10 GARLIC CLOVES, CRUSHED

4 SPRIGS OF FRESH OREGANO

1 SPRIG OF FRESH ROSEMARY

1 TEASPOON PAPRIKA

1 TEASPOON KOSHER SALT

1 TEASPOON BLACK PEPPER

¼ CUP EXTRA-VIRGIN OLIVE OIL

¼ CUP DRY WHITE WINE

2 TABLESPOONS FRESH LEMON JUICE

2½ LBS. BONELESS, SKINLESS CHICKEN THIGHS, CHOPPED

2 BAY LEAVES

PITA BREAD (SEE PAGE 209), WARMED, FOR SERVING

CHICKEN SOUVLAKI

1. Place the garlic, oregano, rosemary, paprika, salt, pepper, olive oil, wine, and lemon juice in a food processor and blitz to combine.

2. Place the chicken and bay leaves in a bowl or a large resealable bag, pour the marinade over the chicken, and let it marinate in the refrigerator for 2 hours.

3. Prepare a gas or charcoal grill, setting up one zone for direct heat and another for indirect.

4. Remove the chicken from the marinade and thread it onto skewers.

5. Place your hand over the grate to test the heat in each section. Place the chicken over medium heat—a spot you can leave your hand over for 5 seconds before you need to move it away. Cook until the chicken is cooked through and the exterior is lightly charred, about 15 minutes, turning the skewers as little as possible.

6. Remove the skewers from heat and let them rest for 2 minutes. Serve with pita and vegetables and herbs of your choice and enjoy.

CHICKEN SOUVLAKI
See page 77

YIELD: 5 TO 10 SERVINGS / **TOTAL TIME:** 2½ TO 3 HOURS

2 TEASPOONS KOSHER SALT

2 TEASPOONS BLACK PEPPER

1 TABLESPOON GARLIC POWDER

1 TABLESPOON ONION POWDER

10 TO 20 LB. TURKEY, GIBLETS AND INNARDS REMOVED

5 TABLESPOONS UNSALTED BUTTER, MELTED

2 TABLESPOONS CHOPPED FRESH HERBS

SPATCHCOCK TURKEY

1. Place the salt, pepper, garlic powder, and onion powder in a bowl and stir to combine. Set the mixture aside.

2. Place the turkey on a cutting board, breast side down. Using kitchen shears, cut out the backbone of the turkey. Flip the turkey back over so the breast side is up and set it on a wire rack placed inside a roasting pan. Push down on the middle of the bird to flatten it as much as possible.

3. Rub the melted butter all over the breast side of the turkey and then rub the salt mixture all over the breast side of the turkey. Sprinkle the herbs over the top and place the turkey in the refrigerator.

4. Prepare a gas or charcoal grill, setting up one zone for direct heat and another for indirect.

5. Place your hand over the grate to test the heat in each section. Place the turkey, breast side down, over medium-low heat—a spot you can leave your hand over for 6 or 7 seconds before you need to move it away. Cook until the interior of the thickest part of the turkey's leg is 165°F and the skin is nice and crispy, turning the turkey just once. The cooking time will depend on the size of the turkey, but plan for anywhere from 1 hour and 15 minutes to 1 hour and 45 minutes.

6. Remove the turkey from heat and let it rest for 20 minutes before slicing and serving.

YIELD: 4 TO 6 SERVINGS / **TOTAL TIME:** 24 HOURS

POULTRY BRINE (SEE PAGE 187)

4 LB. WHOLE CHICKEN

ROTISSERIE CHICKEN

1. Place the brine in a large stockpot and add the chicken. You want to ensure that the entire bird is submerged. If it is not, weigh the chicken down with a few plates. Brine the chicken in the refrigerator overnight.

2. Prepare a gas or charcoal grill for high heat (about 500°F). Set up a rotisserie over the grate.

3. Remove the chicken from the marinade and thread it onto the rotisserie. Cook the chicken until the drumstick breaks away from the bone at the end when you pull up on it or the interior of the thickest part of the thigh is 160°F.

4. Remove the chicken from heat and let it rest for 10 minutes before carving. This period of rest should bring the temperature of the interior up to 165°F.

YIELD: 4 SERVINGS / **TOTAL TIME:** 24 HOURS

4 LB. WHOLE CHICKEN

2 TABLESPOONS EXTRA-VIRGIN OLIVE OIL

¼ CUP ZA'ATAR (SEE PAGE 183)

ZA'ATAR CHICKEN

1. Place a wire rack in a rimmed baking sheet. Place the chicken, breast side down, on a cutting board. Using kitchen shears, cut out the chicken's backbone. Flip the chicken over so the breast side is facing up. Push down on the middle of the chicken to flatten it as much as possible. Pat the chicken dry and place it on the wire rack.

2. Place the chicken in the refrigerator and let it rest, uncovered, overnight.

3. Remove the chicken from the refrigerator and rub it with the olive oil. Sprinkle the Za'atar over the chicken and let it rest at room temperature for 30 minutes.

4. Prepare a gas or charcoal grill, setting up one zone for direct heat and another for indirect.

5. Place your hand over the grate to test the heat in each section. Place the chicken, breast side down, over medium heat—a spot you can leave your hand over for 5 seconds before you need to move it away. Cook until the chicken is very crispy, about 10 minutes. Turn the chicken over and cook until the interior of the thickest part of the thigh is 165°F.

6. Remove the chicken from heat and let it rest for 5 minutes before serving.

YIELD: 6 SERVINGS / **TOTAL TIME:** 2 DAYS

5- TO 6-LB. SKIN-ON PORK BELLY

1 TABLESPOON FINELY CHOPPED FRESH ROSEMARY

1 TABLESPOON FRESH THYME

1 TABLESPOON CHOPPED FRESH SAGE

2 TEASPOONS GARLIC POWDER

SALT, TO TASTE

1-LB. CENTER-CUT PORK TENDERLOIN

PORCHETTA

1. Place the pork belly skin side down on a cutting board. Using a sharp knife, score the flesh in a crosshatch pattern, cutting about ¼ inch deep. Flip the pork belly over and poke small holes in the skin. Turn the pork belly back over and rub the herbs, garlic powder, and salt into the scored flesh. Place the pork tenderloin in the center of the pork belly and then roll the pork belly up so that it retains its length. Tie the rolled pork belly securely with kitchen twine every ½ inch.

2. Transfer the porchetta to a rack set in a large roasting pan, place it in the fridge, and leave it uncovered for 2 days. This allows the skin to dry out a bit. Blot the porchetta occasionally with paper towels to remove excess moisture.

3. Remove the porchetta from the refrigerator and let it stand at room temperature.

4. Prepare a gas or charcoal grill, setting up one zone for direct heat and another for indirect.

5. Place your hand over the grate to test the heat in each section. Place the porchetta over medium-high heat—a spot you can leave your hand over for 3 or 4 seconds before you need to move it away. Cook until the exterior is seared all over, 8 to 10 minutes, turning the porchetta as needed.

6. Move the porchetta over medium-low heat—a spot you can leave your hand over for 6 or 7 seconds before you need to move it away. Cook the porchetta until the interior is 145°F, 1 to 2 hours, turning it as little as possible.

7. Remove the porchetta from heat and let it rest for 15 minutes before slicing and serving.

YIELD: 4 SERVINGS / **TOTAL TIME:** 45 MINUTES

4 BONE-IN PORK CHOPS, EACH 1 TO 1½ INCHES THICK

SALT AND PEPPER, TO TASTE

PORK CHOPS

1. Prepare a gas or charcoal grill, setting up one zone for direct heat and another for indirect.

2. Season the pork chops with salt and pepper. Place your hand over the grate to test the heat in each section. Place the pork chops over medium heat—a spot you can leave your hand over for 5 seconds before you need to move it away. Cook until the interiors are 145°F and the exteriors are nicely seared, 10 to 12 minutes.

3. Remove the pork chops from heat and let them rest for 2 minutes before serving.

PORCHETTA
See page 84

YIELD: 2 SERVINGS / **TOTAL TIME:** 30 MINUTES

2 (½ LB.) PORTIONS OF CENTER-CUT PORK TENDERLOIN

2 TEASPOONS KOSHER SALT, PLUS MORE TO TASTE

1 TEASPOON BLACK PEPPER

1 TEASPOON SMOKED PAPRIKA

1 TEASPOON ONION POWDER

½ TEASPOON GARLIC POWDER

½ TEASPOON CUMIN

½ CUP GREEN GODDESS PESTO (SEE PAGE 214)

GRILLED PORK LOIN
WITH GREEN GODDESS PESTO

1. Prepare a gas or charcoal grill, setting up one zone for direct heat and another for indirect.

2. Pat the pork dry with paper towels. Place the remaining ingredients, except for the pesto, in a bowl, stir to combine, and season the pork with the mixture.

3. Place your hand over the grate to test the heat in each section and place the pork over medium heat—a spot you can leave your hand over for 5 seconds before you need to

   move it away. Cook until the interior is 135°F and it is lightly charred all over, 8 to 10 minutes, turning it as necessary.

4. Remove the pork from the grill and let it rest for 10 minutes, which should bring the interior up to 145°F.

5. Slice the pork, season it with salt, drizzle the pesto over the top, and serve.

YIELD: 4 SERVINGS / **TOTAL TIME:** 1 HOUR AND 30 MINUTES

4 GARLIC CLOVES, MINCED

1 TABLESPOON GRATED FRESH GINGER

½ CUP GOCHUJANG

2 TABLESPOONS SOY SAUCE

3 TABLESPOONS SESAME OIL

2 LBS. PORK TENDERLOIN

SESAME SEEDS, FOR GARNISH

2 SCALLIONS, TRIMMED AND CHOPPED, FOR GARNISH

WHITE RICE, COOKED, FOR SERVING

ROMAINE LETTUCE LEAVES, FOR SERVING

MUSAENGCHAE (SEE PAGE 207), FOR SERVING

DWAEJI BULGOGI

1. Place all of the ingredients, except for the pork and those designated for garnish or for serving, in a bowl and stir to combine. Place the pork in a baking dish, pour the marinade over it, and let the meat marinate in the refrigerator for 1 hour.

2. Prepare a gas or charcoal grill, setting up one zone for direct heat and another for indirect.

3. Remove the pork from the marinade. Place your hand over the grate to test the heat in each section. Place the pork over medium-high heat—a spot you can leave your hand over for 3 or 4 seconds before you need to move it away. Grill until the interior is 145°F and the exterior is nicely seared, 15 to 20 minutes.

4. Remove the pork from heat and let it rest for 5 minutes.

5. Slice the pork thin and garnish it with sesame seeds and the scallions. Serve with white rice, romaine lettuce leaves, and the Musaengchae and enjoy.

LICENSE TO GRILL

YIELD: 6 SERVINGS / **TOTAL TIME:** 2 HOURS AND 30 MINUTES

3 TABLESPOONS EXTRA-VIRGIN OLIVE OIL

1½ CUPS FRESH ORANGE JUICE, STRAINED

2 TEASPOONS ORANGE ZEST

1 GARLIC CLOVE, CHOPPED

2 BAY LEAVES

PINCH OF CHILI POWDER

PINCH OF DRIED OREGANO

2½ LB. PORK TENDERLOIN

SALT AND PEPPER, TO TASTE

SPICY ORANGE PORK

1. Prepare a gas or charcoal grill, setting up one zone for direct heat and another for indirect.

2. Place your hand over the grate to test the heat in each section. Place the olive oil in a large cast-iron skillet and place it over medium-high heat—a spot you can leave your hand over for 3 or 4 seconds before you need to move it away. Gently pour the fresh orange juice into the pan and then stir in the orange zest, garlic, bay leaves, chili powder, and oregano. Let the mixture come to a simmer.

3. Season the pork with salt and pepper and place it in the pan. Braise the pork until it registers 135°F on an instant-read thermometer, about 1½ hours, basting it occasionally.

4. Remove the pork from the pan and place it directly on the grate. Cook until the pork registers 145°F on an instant-read thermometer and the exterior is nicely seared, about 10 minutes, turning it as necessary.

5. Remove the pork from the grill and let it rest for 5 minutes before slicing and serving.

SEAFOOD

Seafood is a natural for the grill, with mildly flavored flesh that eagerly embraces smoke, and a lean character that cooks quickly. These attributes also mean that seafood requires more care, but do not worry— the thorough instructions in this section will teach you how to remain on the right side of the line when handling the delicate fruits of the sea.

YIELD: 6 SERVINGS / **TOTAL TIME:** 45 MINUTES

2 LBS. SALMON FILLETS, SKIN REMOVED

¼ CUP BLACKENING SPICE (SEE PAGE 182)

ZEST OF 1 LEMON

LEMON WEDGES, FOR SERVING

BLACKENED SALMON

1. Prepare a gas or charcoal grill, setting up one zone for direct heat and another for indirect.

2. Rub the salmon with the Blackening Spice. Place your hand over the grate to test the heat in each section. Place the salmon over high heat—a spot you can only leave your hand over for 2 seconds before you need to move it away. Cook for 3 to 4 minutes and turn the salmon over. Cook until the interior of the salmon offers just a little bit of resistance when you squeeze its sides.

3. Remove the salmon from heat, sprinkle the lemon zest over it, and serve with lemon wedges.

YIELD: 4 SERVINGS / **TOTAL TIME:** 40 MINUTES

2 WHOLE RED SNAPPER, SCALED, CLEANED, GUTTED, AND BUTTERFLIED

SALT, TO TASTE

½ TEASPOON DRIED MEXICAN OREGANO

1 TEASPOON CUMIN

3 GUAJILLO CHILE PEPPERS, STEMMED AND SEEDED

2 ANCHO CHILE PEPPERS, STEMMED AND SEEDED

3 GARLIC CLOVES

2 TABLESPOONS MAGGI SEASONING OR WORCESTERSHIRE SAUCE

¼ CUP FRESH LIME JUICE

CORN TORTILLAS (SEE PAGE 208), WARM, FOR SERVING

PESCADO ZARANDEADO

1. Using a sharp knife, score each side of the fish four times. Season them with salt, the oregano, and cumin and place them in a large roasting pan.

2. Place the chile peppers in a bowl of boiling water and let them soak for 10 minutes. Drain the chiles, reserve the soaking liquid, and place the chiles in a blender.

3. Add the garlic and Maggi sauce to the blender and puree until smooth, adding the reserved liquid as needed to get the desired texture.

4. Pour the puree over the fish and let it marinate for 20 minutes.

5. Prepare a gas or charcoal grill, setting up one zone for direct heat and another for indirect. Coat the grate with nonstick cooking spray.

6. Place your hand over the grate to test the heat in each section. Place the fish over high heat—a spot you can only leave your hand over for 2 seconds before you need to move it away. Cook for 3 to 4 minutes and turn the fish over. Cook until the interior of the fish offers just a little bit of resistance when you squeeze its sides.

7. Remove the fish from the grill and pour the lime juice over it. Serve immediately with warm tortillas.

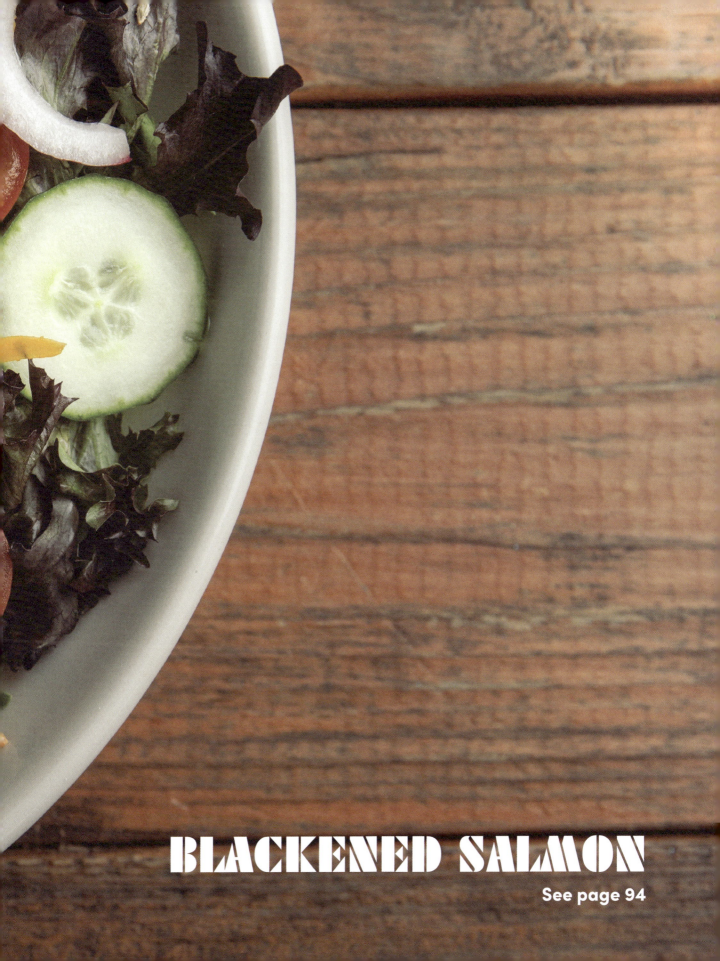

BLACKENED SALMON
See page 94

YIELD: 6 SERVINGS / **TOTAL TIME:** 45 MINUTES

2 CUPS DRY WHITE WINE

2 GARLIC CLOVES, MINCED

2 SHALLOTS, FINELY DICED

¼ CUP CHOPPED FRESH PARSLEY

1 TEASPOON FRESH THYME

6 LBS. MUSSELS, RINSED WELL AND DEBEARDED

SALT, TO TASTE

CRUSTY BREAD, FOR SERVING

MUSSELS
IN WHITE WINE & HERBS

1. Prepare a gas or charcoal grill, setting up one zone for direct heat and another for indirect.

2. Place the wine, garlic, shallots, parsley, and thyme in a stockpot. Place your hand over the grate to test the heat in each section. Place the pot over medium heat—a spot you can leave your hand over for 5 seconds before you need to move it away—and bring the mixture to a simmer.

3. Add the mussels, partially cover the pot, and simmer for 3 to 4 minutes.

4. Stir to coat the mussels with the broth, partially cover the pot again, and cook until the majority of the mussels have opened, about 4 minutes. Discard any mussels that did not open.

5. Divide the mussels among the serving bowls. Strain the broth and season it with salt. Ladle the broth over the mussels and serve with crusty bread.

YIELD: 8 SERVINGS / **TOTAL TIME:** 1 HOUR AND 15 MINUTES

¼ CUP PICKLING SPICES

¼ CUP KOSHER SALT, PLUS MORE TO TASTE

2 TABLESPOONS MUSTARD SEEDS

2 TABLESPOONS BLACK PEPPERCORNS

2 TABLESPOONS RED PEPPER FLAKES

1 TABLESPOON CELERY SEEDS

2 TABLESPOONS GROUND GINGER

2 TEASPOONS DRIED OREGANO

1 HEAD OF GARLIC, SPLIT IN HALF HORIZONTALLY

2 LBS. ANDOUILLE SAUSAGE

2 LBS. RUSSET POTATOES

2 LBS. SHRIMP, SHELLS REMOVED, DEVEINED

2 LEMONS, 1 JUICED; 1 HALVED

¼ CUP EXTRA-VIRGIN OLIVE OIL

FRESH PARSLEY, CHOPPED, FOR GARNISH

REMOULADE SAUCE (SEE PAGE 198), FOR SERVING

SHRIMP BOIL

1. Prepare a gas or charcoal grill, setting up one zone for direct heat and another for indirect.

2. Place the pickling spices, salt, mustard seeds, peppercorns, red pepper flakes, celery seeds, ginger, and oregano in a bowl and stir to combine. Set the seasoning mixture aside.

3. Place 12 cups water in a stockpot. Place your hand over the grate to test the heat in each section. Place the pot over high heat—a spot you can only leave your hand over for 2 seconds before you need to move it away—and bring the water to a boil.

4. Whisk in the seasoning mixture and bring the water back to a rapid simmer. Add the garlic, sausage, and potatoes, return to a simmer, and cover the pot with a lid. Cook until the potatoes are just tender, 10 to 15 minutes.

5. Remove the potatoes and sausage from the pot, place them on a platter, and set them aside. Stir the shrimp and lemon juice into the pot, partially cover the pot, and simmer the shrimp until they are pink and tender, about 5 minutes.

6. While the shrimp are cooking, cut the potatoes into wedges and the sausages in half. Place them in a large mixing bowl, drizzle the olive oil over them, and season with salt. Toss to combine.

7. Place the potatoes and sausages over medium heat—a spot you can leave your hand over for 5 seconds before you need to move it away—and cook until the potatoes are golden brown and the sausages are lightly charred, 5 to 8 minutes, turning them as necessary.

8. Drain the shrimp and arrange them on a platter along with the potatoes, sausage, and lemon halves. Garnish with parsley and serve with the Remoulade Sauce.

YIELD: 4 SERVINGS / **TOTAL TIME:** 45 MINUTES

1½ LBS. TILAPIA FILLETS, EACH ABOUT ¾ INCH THICK

½ CUP UNSALTED BUTTER, MELTED

CAJUN RUB (SEE PAGE 183)

LEMON WEDGES, FOR SERVING

CAJUN TILAPIA

1. Prepare a gas or charcoal grill, setting up one zone for direct heat and another for indirect.

2. Dip the tilapia in the melted butter and then apply the rub until the tilapia is generously coated on both sides.

3. Place your hand over the grate to test the heat in each section. Place the tilapia over high heat—a spot you can only leave your hand over for 2 seconds before you need to move it away. Cook until the tilapia is cooked through and lightly charred, about 6 minutes, turning it over just once. To determine if the inside is cooked enough, squeeze the sides of the tilapia. If the inside offers just a bit of resistance, it is ready.

4. Remove the tilapia from heat, serve with lemon wedges, and enjoy.

YIELD: 2 SERVINGS / **TOTAL TIME:** 45 MINUTES

1 TO 2 LB. WHOLE BRANZINO

4 FRESH BASIL LEAVES

1 TABLESPOON KOSHER SALT

1 TABLESPOON BLACK PEPPER

½ LEMON

WHOLE BRANZINO

1. Prepare a gas or charcoal grill, setting up one zone for direct heat and another for indirect.

2. Clean the branzino, remove the bones, and descale it. Pat it dry with paper towels and rub the flesh with the basil leaves. Season with the salt and pepper and close the fish back up.

3. Place your hand over the grate to test the heat in each section. Place the fish over medium-high heat—a spot you can leave your hand over for 3 or 4 seconds before you need to move it away. Cook until the fish is just cooked through and the skin is crispy, 10 to 12 minutes, turning the fish over just once.

4. Remove the fish from heat and place it on a large platter. Squeeze the lemon over it and enjoy.

WHOLE BRANZINO
See page 103

YIELD: 4 SERVINGS / **TOTAL TIME:** 1 HOUR AND 15 MINUTES

10 OZ. GARLIC CLOVES, UNPEELED

1 CUP PLUS 2 TABLESPOONS UNSALTED BUTTER

2 TABLESPOONS GUAJILLO CHILE POWDER

2 TABLESPOONS CHOPPED FRESH CILANTRO

SALT, TO TASTE

4 FRESH LOBSTER TAILS, SPLIT IN HALF LENGTHWISE SO THAT THE FLESH IS EXPOSED

LIME WEDGES, FOR SERVING

LOBSTER MOJO DE AJO

1. Place the garlic in a dry skillet and toast over medium heat until it is lightly charred in spots, about 10 minutes, turning occasionally. Remove the garlic from the pan and peel it.

2. Place the butter in a clean skillet and melt it over medium heat. Add the garlic and continue cooking until the butter begins to foam and brown slightly. Remove the pan from heat and let the mixture cool to room temperature.

3. Place the butter, garlic, guajillo powder, and cilantro in a blender and puree until smooth. Season with salt and transfer three-quarters of the mojo de ajo to a large mixing bowl. Place the remaining mojo de ajo in a small bowl and set it aside. Let it cool completely.

4. Add the lobster tails to the mojo in the large mixing bowl and let them marinate for 30 minutes.

5. Prepare a gas or charcoal grill, setting up one zone for direct heat and another for indirect.

6. Place the small bowl containing the reserved mojo de ajo beside the fire. Place your hand over the grate to test the heat in each section. Place the lobster tails, flesh side down, over high heat—a spot you can only leave your hand over for 2 seconds before you need to move it away. Cook until the flesh is caramelized and almost cooked through, 3 to 4 minutes.

7. Turn the lobster tails over and brush them with some of the reserved mojo de ajo. Cook until they are completely cooked through, 1 to 2 minutes.

8. Remove the lobster tails from heat and serve with lime wedges and any of the remaining reserved mojo de ajo.

YIELD: 4 TO 6 SERVINGS / **TOTAL TIME:** 3 HOURS

1 HEAD OF GARLIC, HALVED

1 WHITE ONION, QUARTERED

3 ALLSPICE BERRIES

2 WHOLE CLOVES

½ CINNAMON STICK

3 CHIPOTLE MORITA CHILE PEPPERS

2 DRIED CHILES DE ÀRBOL

7 GUAJILLO CHILE PEPPERS

2 TABLESPOONS FRESH LIME JUICE

2 TABLESPOONS ORANGE JUICE

2 TABLESPOONS GRAPEFRUIT JUICE

7 TABLESPOONS PINEAPPLE JUICE

½ CUP RECADO ROJO (SEE PAGE 193)

5 GARLIC CLOVES

⅛ TEASPOON DRIED OREGANO

SALT, TO TASTE

6 LB. OCTOPUS, BEAK REMOVED AND HEAD CLEANED

1 SMALL BUNCH OF FRESH EPAZOTE

3 BAY LEAVES

8 CUPS CHICKEN STOCK (SEE PAGE 215)

CORN TORTILLAS (SEE PAGE 208), FOR SERVING

LIME WEDGES, FOR SERVING

OCTOPUS AL PASTOR

1. Place the head of garlic and onion in a dry skillet and cook them over medium heat until they are lightly charred. Remove them from the pan and set them aside.

2. Add the allspice, cloves, and cinnamon stick to the skillet and toast until fragrant, shaking the pan frequently. Grind the spices into a powder using a mortar and pestle or a spice grinder.

3. Place the chiles in the skillet and toast over medium heat until they darken and become fragrant and pliable. Submerge them in a bowl of hot water and let them soak for 30 minutes.

4. Drain the chiles and reserve the liquid. Add the chiles, toasted spice powder, juices, Recado Rojo, garlic cloves (not the charred head of garlic), and oregano to a blender and puree until smooth, adding the reserved liquid as necessary to get the desired texture. Season the al pastor marinade with salt and set it aside.

5. Preheat the oven to 275°F. Bring water to a boil in a large saucepan. Place the octopus in the boiling water and poach it for 3 minutes. Remove the octopus from the water and let it cool.

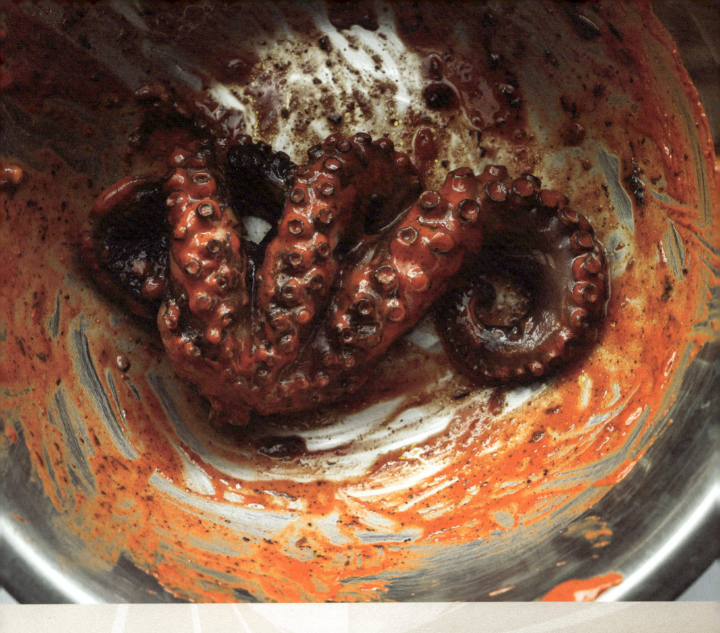

6. Place the octopus, epazote, bay leaves, head of garlic, and onion in a Dutch oven and add the stock until half of the octopus is submerged. Cover the Dutch oven and place it in the oven. Braise the octopus for 2 to 3 hours, until the thickest parts of the tentacles are very tender. Remove the octopus from the braising liquid and let it cool.

7. Prepare a gas or charcoal grill, setting up one zone for direct heat and another for indirect.

8. Place your hand over the grate to test the heat in each section. Place the octopus over high heat—a spot you can only leave your hand over for 2 seconds before you need to move it away. Cook until it is caramelized and crispy all over, about 5 to 7 minutes.

9. Remove the octopus from heat and serve it with tortillas and lime wedges.

YIELD: 4 SERVINGS / **TOTAL TIME:** 45 MINUTES

2 TABLESPOONS HONEY

¼ CUP SOY SAUCE

2 LARGE RAINBOW TROUT FILLETS, SKIN REMOVED

SALT AND PEPPER, TO TASTE

1 LIME, HALVED

SESAME SEEDS, FOR GARNISH

HONEY & SOY-GLAZED RAINBOW TROUT

1. Prepare a gas or charcoal grill, setting up one zone for direct heat and another for indirect.

2. Place the honey and soy sauce in a small bowl and stir until the honey has liquefied. Divide the glaze into two portions.

3. Place the trout on a plate, season it with salt and pepper, and brush it with half of the glaze. Place your hand over the grate to test the heat in each section. Place the trout over medium-high heat—a spot you can leave your hand over for 3 or 4 seconds before you need to move it away. Cook until the trout is cooked through and the exterior is lightly charred, about 6 minutes, turning it over just once. To determine if the inside is cooked enough, squeeze the sides of the trout. If the inside offers just a bit of resistance, it is ready.

4. Remove the trout from heat and place it on a platter. Spoon the remaining glaze over the trout and squeeze the lime over the top. Garnish the dish with sesame seeds and enjoy.

YIELD: 4 SERVINGS / **TOTAL TIME:** 1 HOUR AND 15 MINUTES

- 2 LBS. JUMBO SHRIMP, SHELLS REMOVED, DEVEINED
- 1 TEASPOON CAYENNE PEPPER
- 1 TEASPOON DRIED THYME
- 1 TEASPOON DRIED OREGANO
- 1 TEASPOON SWEET PAPRIKA
- 1 TEASPOON DRIED ROSEMARY
- 1 TEASPOON GARLIC POWDER
- 2 TABLESPOONS CHOPPED FRESH PARSLEY, PLUS MORE FOR GARNISH
- 1 TEASPOON KOSHER SALT
- 1 TEASPOON BLACK PEPPER
- 2 TABLESPOONS EXTRA-VIRGIN OLIVE OIL
- LIME WEDGES, FOR SERVING

BBQ SHRIMP, NEW ORLEANS STYLE

1. Pat the shrimp dry with paper towels and place them in a large mixing bowl. Set the shrimp aside.

2. Place the cayenne, thyme, oregano, paprika, rosemary, garlic powder, parsley, salt, and pepper in a mixing bowl and stir until well combined. Sprinkle the mixture over the shrimp and toss to coat.

3. Drizzle the olive oil over the shrimp and toss to coat. Cover the bowl with plastic wrap and let the shrimp marinate in the refrigerator for 40 minutes.

4. Prepare a gas or charcoal grill, setting up one zone for direct heat and another for indirect.

5. Thread the shrimp onto skewers. Place your hand over the grate to test the heat in each section. Place the skewers over high heat—a spot you can only leave your hand over for 2 seconds before you need to move it away. Cook until the shrimp turn pink and are cooked through, 3 to 5 minutes, turning them as necessary.

6. Remove the skewers from heat and garnish them with additional parsley. Serve with lime wedges and enjoy.

BBQ SHRIMP
See page 111

YIELD: 4 SERVINGS / **TOTAL TIME:** 1 HOUR

3½ TABLESPOONS FRESH LIME JUICE

2 GARLIC CLOVES, MINCED

1 BUNCH OF FRESH PARSLEY, CHOPPED

2 TABLESPOONS EXTRA-VIRGIN OLIVE OIL

SALT AND PEPPER, TO TASTE

1 LB. SALMON FILLETS, SKIN REMOVED, CUT INTO LARGE CUBES

2 CELERY STALKS, CUT INTO 1-INCH PIECES

1 YELLOW BELL PEPPER, STEMMED, SEEDED, AND CUT INTO 1-INCH PIECES

16 CHERRY TOMATOES

LIME WEDGES, FOR SERVING

SALMON & VEGETABLE SKEWERS

1. Place the lime juice, garlic, parsley, olive oil, salt, and pepper in a large bowl and stir until well combined. Add the salmon, celery, bell pepper, and tomatoes and toss until well coated. Cover the bowl with plastic wrap and let the mixture marinate in the refrigerator for 30 minutes.

2. Prepare a gas or charcoal grill, setting up one zone for direct heat and another for indirect.

3. Thread the salmon, celery, bell pepper, and tomatoes onto skewers, alternating between them.

4. Place your hand over the grate to test the heat in each section. Place the skewers over medium-high heat—a spot you can leave your hand over for 3 or 4 seconds before you need to move it away. Cook until the salmon is cooked through and the vegetables are tender, 8 to 10 minutes, turning the skewers as little as possible.

5. Remove the skewers from heat, serve with lime wedges, and enjoy.

YIELD: 6 SERVINGS / **TOTAL TIME:** 3 HOURS

2 TABLESPOONS WHOLE-GRAIN MUSTARD

2 TABLESPOONS MILD HONEY OR PURE MAPLE SYRUP

1 TEASPOON FINELY CHOPPED FRESH ROSEMARY

1 TABLESPOON LEMON ZEST

½ TEASPOON KOSHER SALT

½ TEASPOON BLACK PEPPER

2 LB. SKIN-ON SALMON FILLET (ABOUT 1½ INCHES THICK)

CEDAR-PLANK SALMON

1. Soak a cedar grilling plank in water for 2 hours.

2. Prepare a gas or charcoal grill, setting up one zone for direct heat and another for indirect.

3. Place the mustard, honey, rosemary, lemon zest, salt, and pepper in a bowl and stir until well combined. Spread the mixture over the salmon and let it stand at room temperature for 15 minutes.

4. Place the salmon on the plank, skin side down. Place your hand over the grate to test the heat in each section. Place the plank over medium-high heat—a spot you can leave your hand over for 3 or 4 seconds before you need to move it away. Cook until the salmon is just cooked through and the edges are browned, 13 to 15 minutes.

5. Remove the salmon from the grill and let it rest on the plank for 3 minutes before serving.

CEDAR-PLANK SALMON
See page 115

YIELD: 4 SERVINGS / **TOTAL TIME:** 1 HOUR AND 15 MINUTES

FOR THE TUNA

3½ TABLESPOONS ORANGE JUICE

3½ TABLESPOONS SOY SAUCE

1 TABLESPOON FRESH LEMON JUICE

2 TABLESPOONS EXTRA-VIRGIN OLIVE OIL

2 TABLESPOONS CHOPPED FRESH PARSLEY

1 GARLIC CLOVE, MINCED

½ TEASPOON CHOPPED FRESH OREGANO

½ TEASPOON BLACK PEPPER

1 LB. TUNA STEAKS

FOR THE SALAD

4 ORANGES

2 SMALL FENNEL BULBS, TRIMMED AND SLICED THIN

½ RED ONION, SLICED THIN

1 CUP MESCLUN GREENS

2 TABLESPOONS FRESH LEMON JUICE

1 TABLESPOON SOY SAUCE

3½ TABLESPOONS EXTRA-VIRGIN OLIVE OIL

SALT AND PEPPER, TO TASTE

TUNA
WITH ORANGE & FENNEL SALAD

1. To begin preparations for the tuna, place the orange juice, soy sauce, lemon juice, olive oil, parsley, garlic, oregano, and pepper in a baking dish. Place the tuna steaks in the marinade and turn until they are coated. Cover the dish with plastic wrap and marinate the tuna in the refrigerator for 1 hour.

2. To prepare the salad, peel the oranges and remove all of the white pith. Segment the oranges and reserve any juice. Place the orange segments, fennel, onion, and greens in a large bowl and toss to combine. Place the lemon juice, soy sauce, reserved orange juice, and olive oil in a small bowl, season the mixture with salt and pepper, and whisk until the dressing has emulsified. Drizzle the dressing over the salad and toss to coat. Set the salad aside.

3. Prepare a gas or charcoal grill, setting up one zone for direct heat and another for indirect.

4. Place your hand over the grate to test the heat in each section. Place the tuna over high heat—a spot you can only leave your hand over for 2 seconds before you need to move it away. Grill until both sides of the tuna are seared and the interior is rare, about 1 minute per side.

5. Remove the tuna from heat and serve it alongside the salad.

LICENSE TO GRILL

YIELD: 6 SERVINGS / **TOTAL TIME:** 1 HOUR

6 SEA BASS FILLETS, SKIN REMOVED, EACH ABOUT ¾ INCH THICK

3 TABLESPOONS RED CHERMOULA SAUCE (SEE PAGE 196)

LEMON WEDGES, FOR SERVING

CHERMOULA SEA BASS

1. Rub the sea bass with the Chermoula Sauce. Place the sea bass in a baking dish and let it marinate in the refrigerator for 30 minutes.

2. Prepare a gas or charcoal grill, setting up one zone for direct heat and another for indirect.

3. Place your hand over the grate to test the heat in each section. Place the sea bass over high heat—a spot you can only leave your hand over for 2 seconds before you need to move it away. Cook until the sea bass is just cooked through and lightly charred, about 6 minutes, turning it over just once. To determine if the inside is cooked enough, squeeze the sides of the sea bass. If the inside offers just a bit of resistance, it is ready.

4. Remove the sea bass from heat, let it rest for 2 minutes, and serve with lemon wedges.

YIELD: 4 SERVINGS / **TOTAL TIME:** 50 MINUTES

4 SWORDFISH STEAKS, EACH ABOUT ¾ TO 1 INCH THICK

1½ TABLESPOONS EXTRA-VIRGIN OLIVE OIL

SEAFOOD RUB (SEE PAGE 177), TO TASTE

LEMON WEDGES, FOR SERVING

SWORDFISH

1. Prepare a gas or charcoal grill, setting up one zone for direct heat and another for indirect.

2. Rub the swordfish with the olive oil and then apply the rub until it is generously coated on both sides and let it rest at room temperature for 20 minutes.

3. Place your hand over the grate to test the heat in each section. Place the swordfish over medium-high heat—a spot you can leave your hand over for 3 or 4 seconds before you need to move it away. Cook until the swordfish is just cooked through and the exterior is nicely seared, about 6 minutes, turning it over just once. To determine if the inside is cooked enough, squeeze the sides of the swordfish. If the inside offers just a bit of resistance, it is ready.

4. Remove the swordfish from heat, let it rest for 2 minutes, and serve with lemon wedges.

APPETIZERS, SIDES & SALADS

Whether it be a light appetizer to invigorate the palate, a wholesome salad to temper a heavy entree, or a side that features the fruits of your labors in the garden, these recipes are sure to round out your table, and improve your skills on the grill.

YIELD: 4 SERVINGS / **TOTAL TIME:** 45 MINUTES

1 CANTALOUPE

1 TABLESPOON EXTRA-VIRGIN OLIVE OIL

4 OZ. FRESH MOZZARELLA CHEESE, TORN

1 TABLESPOON BALSAMIC GLAZE (SEE PAGE 213)

FRESH PARSLEY, CHOPPED, FOR GARNISH

CANTALOUPE & MOZZARELLA
WITH BALSAMIC GLAZE

1. Remove the rind from the cantaloupe, halve it, remove the seeds, and then cut the cantaloupe into ½-inch-thick slices. Set the cantaloupe aside.

2. Prepare a gas or charcoal grill, setting up one zone for direct heat and another for indirect.

3. Place the cantaloupe in a mixing bowl, add the olive oil, and toss to coat.

4. Place your hand over the grate to test the heat in each section. Place the cantaloupe over medium-high heat—a spot you can leave your hand over for 3 or 4 seconds before you need to move it away. Grill until the cantaloupe is lightly charred on both sides and warmed through, 4 to 6 minutes.

5. To serve, pile the warm cantaloupe on a plate, top with the mozzarella, and drizzle the Balsamic Glaze over the top. Garnish with parsley and enjoy.

YIELD: 2 SERVINGS / **TOTAL TIME:** 30 MINUTES

1 CUP PINOT NOIR

¼ CUP SUGAR

4 ORANGE SLICES

6 FRESH FIGS, HALVED

2 TABLESPOONS CRUMBLED GOAT CHEESE

FIG & GOAT CHEESE SALAD

1. Prepare a gas or charcoal grill, setting up one zone for direct heat and another for indirect.

2. Place the wine and sugar in a small saucepan and warm the mixture over medium-high heat, stirring until the sugar has dissolved. Simmer until the mixture has reduced to a syrupy consistency. Remove the pan from heat and set it aside.

3. Place your hand over the grate to test the heat in each section. Place the orange slices over medium-high heat—a spot you can leave your hand over for 3 or 4 seconds before you need to move it away. Cook until the orange slices are caramelized on each side, about 2 minutes. Remove them from the grill and set them aside.

4. Place the figs on the grill, cut side down, and cook until they are lightly browned and soft, about 4 minutes.

5. To serve, place the orange slices on a plate, place the figs on top of the orange slices, and sprinkle the goat cheese over the dish. Drizzle the reduction over the top and enjoy.

APPETIZERS, SIDES & SALADS

YIELD: 4 SERVINGS / **TOTAL TIME:** 2 DAYS

2 STAR ANISE PODS

½ CINNAMON STICK

2 DRIED CHILES DE ÁRBOL

2¼ CUPS APPLE CIDER VINEGAR

7 TABLESPOONS WHITE VINEGAR

3 TABLESPOONS SUGAR

SALT, TO TASTE

1 PINEAPPLE, PEELED, CORED, AND SLICED

PICKLED GRILLED PINEAPPLE

1. Prepare a gas or charcoal grill, setting up one zone for direct heat and another for indirect.

2. Place the star anise, cinnamon stick, and chiles in a saucepan and toast until they are fragrant, about 2 minutes, shaking the pan frequently. Add the vinegars and sugar, generously season with salt, and bring to a boil, stirring to dissolve the sugar.

3. Pour the brine into a sterilized mason jar and set it aside.

4. Place your hand over the grate to test the heat in each section. Place the pineapple over medium-high heat—a spot you can leave your hand over for 3 to 4 seconds before you need to move it away. Cook until it is charred on both sides, about 8 minutes, turning it over halfway through.

5. Remove the pineapple from the grill and add it to the brine while it is still warm. Let the mixture cool to room temperature, cover the jar, and let the pineapple pickle in the refrigerator for 2 days before using.

LICENSE TO GRILL

YIELD: 4 SERVINGS / **TOTAL TIME:** 30 MINUTES

1 EAR OF CORN, HUSK ON

1 OZ. PUMPKIN SEEDS

1 OZ. POMEGRANATE SEEDS

FLESH OF 3 AVOCADOS

½ RED ONION, CHOPPED

½ CUP CHOPPED FRESH CILANTRO

1 TEASPOON FRESH LIME JUICE

SALT AND PEPPER, TO TASTE

SWEET CORN & PEPITA GUACAMOLE

1. Prepare a gas or charcoal grill, setting up one zone for direct heat and another for indirect.

2. Place your hand over the grate to test the heat in each section. Place the corn over medium-high heat—a spot you can leave your hand over for 3 to 4 seconds before you need to move it away. Cook until it is charred all over and the kernels have softened enough that there is considerable give in them.

3. Remove the corn from the grill and let it cool. When cool enough to handle, husk the corn and cut off the kernels.

4. Combine the corn, pumpkin seeds, and pomegranate seeds in a small bowl. Place the avocados in a separate bowl and mash until just slightly chunky.

5. Stir in the corn mixture, onion, cilantro, and lime juice, season the mixture with salt and pepper, and work the mixture until the guacamole is the desired texture.

SWEET CORN & PEPITA GUACAMOLE

See page 127

YIELD: 6 SERVINGS / **TOTAL TIME:** 1 HOUR AND 30 MINUTES

6 LARGE POBLANO CHILE PEPPERS

1 LB. OAXACA OR MONTEREY JACK CHEESE

4 EGG WHITES

4 EGG YOLKS

2 CUPS ALL-PURPOSE FLOUR

2 CUPS CANOLA OIL

2 LARGE TOMATOES

2 GARLIC CLOVES

¼ WHITE ONION

SALT, TO TASTE

1 TEASPOON DRIED MEXICAN OREGANO

CHILES RELLENOS

1. Prepare a gas or charcoal grill, setting up one zone for direct heat and another for indirect.

2. Place your hand over the grate to test the heat in each section. Place the poblanos over medium-high heat—a spot you can leave your hand over for 3 to 4 seconds before you need to move it away. Cook until they are charred all over, turning them as necessary.

3. Remove the poblanos from the grill, place them in a bowl, cover it with plastic wrap, and let them steam for 5 minutes.

4. Remove the poblanos from the bowl and remove the charred skin with your hands. Using a sharp paring knife, make a cut close to the stems of the peppers. Remove the seed pod, but leave the stems attached.

5. Stuff the poblanos with 1 to 2 oz. of cheese (the amount depends on the size of the chile) and use toothpicks to close up the small cuts you've made.

6. In the work bowl of a stand mixer fitted with the whisk attachment, add the egg whites and whip on high until they hold stiff peaks.

7. Add the egg yolks, reduce the speed to low, and beat until just incorporated, about 30 seconds. Add ½ cup of flour and again beat until just incorporated, as you do not want to overwork the batter.

8. Place the canola oil in a large, deep skillet and warm it to 325°F.

9. Bring water to a boil in a medium saucepan. Add the tomatoes, garlic, and onion and cook until tender, about 7 minutes. Drain, place the vegetables in a blender, and puree until smooth. Season the sauce with salt, stir in the oregano, and set the sauce aside.

10. Place the remaining flour on a baking sheet. Dredge the poblanos in the flour until they are completely coated. Dip the poblanos into the batter until they are coated and gently slip them into the hot oil.

11. Fry the poblanos until they are crispy and golden brown, about 5 minutes, making sure you turn them just once. Transfer the fried peppers to a paper towel–lined plate to drain.

12. When all of the poblanos have been fried, serve them alongside the tomato sauce.

YIELD: 2 TO 4 SERVINGS / **TOTAL TIME:** 3 HOURS

FOR THE CHICKEN WINGS

2 LBS. CHICKEN WINGS

¼ CUP JERK SPICE RUB (SEE PAGE 186)

SALT, TO TASTE

FOR THE SAUCE

1 CUP KETCHUP

1 TABLESPOON JERK SPICE BLEND

1 TEASPOON FRESH LIME JUICE

2 TEASPOONS HOT SAUCE

2 TEASPOONS BROWN SUGAR

JERK CHICKEN WINGS

1. To begin preparations for the chicken wings, poke holes all over the chicken wings with a fork. Place them in a bowl, add the Jerk Spice Rub, and toss to combine. Place the chicken in the refrigerator and let it marinate for 2 hours.

2. Prepare a gas or charcoal grill, setting up one zone for direct heat and another for indirect.

3. To prepare the sauce, place all of the ingredients in a bowl and whisk until well combined. Set the sauce aside.

4. Place your hand over the grate to test the heat in each section. Place the wings over medium heat—a spot you can leave your hand over for 5 seconds before you need to move it away. Cook until they are lightly charred all over and cooked through, 12 to 15 minutes, turning them over once.

5. Remove the wings from the grill and season with salt. Drizzle the sauce over the chicken wings or serve it alongside as a dipping sauce.

JERK CHICKEN WINGS

See page 131

YIELD: 2 TO 4 SERVINGS / **TOTAL TIME:** 30 MINUTES

SALT AND PEPPER, TO TASTE

2 CROWNS OF BROCCOLI, QUARTERED

LEMON & PARMESAN VINAIGRETTE (SEE PAGE 210)

½ CUP PICKLED RED ONION (SEE PAGE 214), FOR GARNISH

½ CUP TOASTED PINE NUTS, FOR GARNISH

CHARRED BROCCOLI WITH LEMON & PARMESAN VINAIGRETTE

1. Prepare a gas or charcoal grill, setting up one zone for direct heat and another for indirect.

2. Bring water to a boil in a large saucepan and prepare an ice bath. Add salt and the broccoli and cook for 1 minute. Remove the broccoli with a strainer and plunge it into the ice bath. Drain the broccoli and let it dry on a paper towel–lined plate.

3. Place your hand over the grate to test the heat in each section. Season the broccoli with salt and pepper and place it over medium-high heat—a spot you can leave your hand over for 3 to 4 seconds before you need to move it away. Cook until it is lightly charred all over, turning it as necessary.

4. Spread the vinaigrette over a serving dish, arrange the broccoli on top, garnish with the pickled onion and toasted pine nuts, and serve.

APPETIZERS, SIDES & SALADS

YIELD: 2 TO 4 SERVINGS / **TOTAL TIME:** 35 MINUTES

4 PEACHES, HALVED AND PITTED

2 TABLESPOONS EXTRA-VIRGIN OLIVE OIL

SALT AND PEPPER, TO TASTE

6 OZ. CILIEGINE MOZZARELLA CHEESE

½ CUP PISTACHIOS, TOASTED

1 CUP CHERRY TOMATOES, HALVED

LEMON & HONEY VINAIGRETTE (SEE PAGE 211)

FRESH BASIL, FOR GARNISH

PEACH SALAD
WITH LEMON & HONEY VINAIGRETTE

1. Prepare a gas or charcoal grill, setting up one zone for direct heat and another for indirect.

2. Brush the cut sides of the peaches with the olive oil and season them with salt and pepper. Place your hand over the grate to test the heat in each section and place the peaches over medium-high heat—a spot you can leave your hand over for 3 to 4 seconds before you need to move it away. Cook until they are lightly charred all over and have softened, 2 to 5 minutes.

3. Remove the peaches from the grill and let them cool.

4. Place the mozzarella, pistachios, and tomatoes in a bowl, add some of the vinaigrette, and toss to combine.

5. Arrange the peaches and mozzarella mixture on a serving platter, drizzle the remaining vinaigrette over the salad, garnish with basil, and serve.

YIELD: 2 SERVINGS / **TOTAL TIME:** 45 MINUTES

½ LB. GOAT CHEESE, SLICED INTO 10 ROUNDS

10 TABLESPOONS EXTRA-VIRGIN OLIVE OIL

1 TEASPOON RED WINE VINEGAR

1 CUP SALT-CURED BLACK OLIVES, PITTED, PATTED DRY, AND CHOPPED

¼ CUP CHOPPED WALNUTS

RED PEPPER FLAKES, TO TASTE

2 TEASPOONS CHOPPED FRESH OREGANO

1 BAGUETTE, SLICED

SALT AND PEPPER, TO TASTE

GRILLED GOAT CHEESE

1. Place the goat cheese on a plate and chill it in the freezer.

2. Place ½ cup of olive oil, the red wine vinegar, olives, walnuts, red pepper flakes, and oregano in a bowl and stir to combine. Set the mixture aside.

3. Prepare a gas or charcoal grill, setting up one zone for direct heat and another for indirect.

4. Place your hand over the grate to test the heat in each section. Place a large cast-iron skillet over high heat—a spot you can only leave your hand over for 2 seconds before you need to move it away. Let the pan warm up for 10 minutes.

5. Brush both sides of the sliced baguette with some of the remaining olive oil. Place the baguette over medium-low heat—a spot you can leave your hand over for 6 or 7 seconds before you need to move it away. Toast the bread until lightly charred on both sides, 5 to 7 minutes. Remove the baguette from heat and set it aside.

6. Place the goat cheese in a single layer in the hot pan and cook until brown and crusty on the bottom, about 2 minutes. Carefully remove the goat cheese from the pan and arrange the rounds on the grilled slices of baguette. Spoon the olive mixture over the cheese, season with salt and pepper, and enjoy.

LICENSE TO GRILL

YIELD: 6 SERVINGS / **TOTAL TIME:** 1 HOUR

FRESH SARDINES, SCALED, GUTTED, AND CLEANED

JUICE OF 2 LEMONS

¼ CUP EXTRA-VIRGIN OLIVE OIL

3 GARLIC CLOVES, MINCED

1 SMALL SHALLOT, MINCED

2 TABLESPOONS CHOPPED FRESH PARSLEY

1 TABLESPOON FRESH CILANTRO

SALT AND PEPPER, TO TASTE

GRILLED SARDINES
WITH LEMON & HERBS

1. Arrange the sardines in a small baking dish. Drizzle the lemon juice and olive oil over them, place them in the refrigerator, and let them marinate for 30 minutes.

2. Prepare a gas or charcoal grill, setting up one zone for direct heat and another for indirect.

3. Place the garlic, shallot, parsley, and cilantro in a small bowl and stir to combine. Stuff the sardines with the mixture, season them with salt and pepper, and thread them onto skewers.

4. Place your hand over the grate to test the heat in each section. Place the skewered sardines over medium heat—a spot you can leave your hand over for 5 seconds before you need to move it away. Cook until they are charred on both sides and their flesh is opaque, around 4 minutes, turning them over just once.

5. Remove the sardines from heat and let them rest for 2 minutes before enjoying.

GRILLED SARDINES
See page 139

YIELD: 2 TO 4 SERVINGS / **TOTAL TIME:** 30 MINUTES

2 HEADS OF RADICCHIO, QUARTERED

1 TABLESPOON EXTRA-VIRGIN OLIVE OIL

1 TABLESPOON FRESH LEMON JUICE

2 TABLESPOONS CHOPPED FRESH PARSLEY

1 TABLESPOON CHOPPED FRESH DILL

TAHINI & DILL CAESAR DRESSING (SEE PAGE 211)

PARMESAN CHEESE, SHAVED, FOR GARNISH

LEMON ZEST, FOR GARNISH

TOASTED SESAME SEEDS, FOR GARNISH

CROUTONS, FOR GARNISH

RADICCHIO
WITH TAHINI & DILL CAESAR DRESSING

1. Prepare a gas or charcoal grill, setting up one zone for direct heat and another for indirect.

2. Place the radicchio, olive oil, lemon juice, parsley, and dill in a mixing bowl and toss to combine.

3. Place your hand over the grate to test the heat in each section and place the radicchio over medium-high heat—a spot you can leave your hand over for 3 to 4 seconds before you need to move it away. Cook until it is tender and lightly charred, turning it as necessary.

4. Remove the radicchio from the grill and place it in a serving dish. Drizzle the dressing over it, garnish with Parmesan, lemon zest, toasted sesame seeds, and croutons, and serve.

APPETIZERS, SIDES & SALADS

YIELD: 4 TO 6 SERVINGS / **TOTAL TIME:** 3 HOURS

2 LBS. CHICKEN WINGS, SEPARATED INTO DRUMETTES AND FLATS

2 TABLESPOONS EXTRA-VIRGIN OLIVE OIL

JUICE OF ½ LIME

3 GARLIC CLOVES, MINCED

2 TABLESPOONS CHOPPED FRESH PARSLEY

1 TABLESPOON CUMIN

2 TEASPOONS SMOKED PAPRIKA

1 TEASPOON CINNAMON

1 TEASPOON TURMERIC

1 TEASPOON RED PEPPER FLAKES

½ TEASPOON ONION POWDER

SALT AND PEPPER, TO TASTE

SMOKY & SPICY CHICKEN WINGS

1. Place the chicken wings on a baking sheet, poke holes in them with a fork, and put them in the refrigerator. Let them rest for at least 2 hours so that the skin on the wings tightens, which will promote crispy wings.

2. Place the wings in a large bowl, add the olive oil, and toss to coat. Place all of the remaining ingredients in another bowl, add the wings, and toss until they are evenly coated.

3. Prepare a gas or charcoal grill, setting up one zone for direct heat and another for indirect.

4. Place your hand over the grate to test the heat in each section. Place the wings over medium-low heat—a spot you can leave your hand over for 6 or 7 seconds before you need to move it away. Cook for 20 minutes.

5. Turn the wings over and cook until they are cooked through and crispy, about 8 minutes.

6. Remove the wings from the grate and enjoy.

YIELD: 4 SERVINGS / **TOTAL TIME:** 3 HOURS

2 LBS. CHICKEN WINGS, SPLIT

2 TABLESPOONS CLARIFIED BUTTER
(SEE PAGE 216)

3 GARLIC CLOVES, MINCED

¼ TEASPOON CAYENNE PEPPER

¼ TEASPOON PAPRIKA

2 TEASPOONS TABASCO

¼ CUP FRANK'S HOT SAUCE

CELERY, CUT INTO 3-INCH PIECES,
FOR SERVING

BUFFALO WINGS

1. Place the chicken wings in a roasting pan, poke them all over with a fork, and place them in the refrigerator. Chill for at least 2 hours so that the skin on the chicken wings tightens, which will promote a crisper wing.

2. Place the Clarified Butter in a saucepan and warm it over medium heat. Add the garlic and cook, stirring continually, for 1 minute. Stir in the cayenne, paprika, Tabasco, and hot sauce and bring to a simmer over medium heat. Simmer for 3 minutes. Transfer the sauce to a mixing bowl and set it aside.

3. Prepare a gas or charcoal grill, setting up one zone for direct heat and another for indirect.

4. Remove the chicken wings from the refrigerator, place them in the buffalo sauce, and toss to coat.

5. Place your hand over the grate to test the heat in each section. Place the chicken wings over medium-high heat—a spot you can leave your hand over for 3 or 4 seconds before you need to move it away. Cook the chicken wings until they are crispy and cooked through, 3 to 5 minutes per side.

6. Remove the wings from the grill, place them on a large serving platter, and serve alongside celery.

APPETIZERS, SIDES & SALADS

YIELD: 2 SERVINGS / **TOTAL TIME:** 30 MINUTES

SALT AND PEPPER, TO TASTE

4 BABY BOK CHOY, TRIMMED AND HALVED LENGTHWISE

2 TABLESPOONS EXTRA-VIRGIN OLIVE OIL

2 CUPS OYSTER MUSHROOMS, SLICED

1 RED BELL PEPPER, STEMMED, SEEDED, AND SLICED

1 SMALL ONION, SLICED

½ CUP SALSA MACHA (SEE PAGE 205)

BABY BOK CHOY
WITH SALSA MACHA

1. Bring water to a boil in a large saucepan and prepare an ice bath. Add salt and the bok choy and cook until it is just tender, about 2 minutes. Drain the bok choy, plunge it into the ice bath, and drain again. Transfer the bok choy to a paper towel–lined plate and let it dry.

2. Prepare a gas or charcoal grill, setting up one zone for direct heat and another for indirect.

3. Place the olive oil in a large skillet and warm it over medium heat. Add the mushrooms, season them with salt and pepper, and cook, stirring occasionally, until they are browned, 10 to 12 minutes.

4. Add the bell pepper and onion and cook, stirring occasionally, until they are tender, about 8 minutes. Remove the pan from heat and set the mixture aside.

5. Place your hand over the grate to test the heat in each section and place the bok choy over high heat—a spot you can only leave your hand over for 2 seconds before you need to move it away. Cook until it is lightly charred, turning it as necessary.

6. Transfer the bok choy and mushroom mixture to a serving dish and toss to combine. Drizzle the Salsa Macha over the top and serve.

YIELD: 4 SERVINGS / **TOTAL TIME:** 1 HOUR AND 30 MINUTES

¼ CUP EXTRA-VIRGIN OLIVE OIL

2 TEASPOONS DIJON MUSTARD

2 GARLIC CLOVES, MINCED

2 TEASPOONS RED WINE VINEGAR

2 TEASPOONS HONEY

1 TEASPOON CHOPPED FRESH ROSEMARY

SALT AND PEPPER, TO TASTE

2 PORTOBELLO MUSHROOMS, STEMMED AND CUT INTO 1-INCH CUBES

2 ZUCCHINI, CUT INTO 1-INCH CUBES

1 RED BELL PEPPER, STEMMED, SEEDED, AND CUT INTO 1-INCH SQUARES

1 GREEN BELL PEPPER, STEMMED, SEEDED, AND CUT INTO 1-INCH SQUARES

VEGETABLE KEBABS

1. Place the olive oil, mustard, garlic, vinegar, honey, and rosemary in a mixing bowl and whisk to combine. Season the dressing with salt and pepper and set it aside.

2. Thread the vegetables onto skewers and place them on a baking sheet. Pour the dressing over the skewers, cover them with plastic wrap, and let them marinate at room temperature for 1 hour, turning occasionally.

3. Prepare a gas or charcoal grill, setting up one zone for direct heat and another for indirect.

4. Remove the vegetable skewers from the dressing and reserve the dressing. Place your hand over the grate to test the heat in each section. Place the kebabs over medium heat—a spot you can leave your hand over for 5 seconds before you need to move it away. Grill until the vegetables are tender and lightly charred, 10 to 12 minutes, turning them as little as possible.

5. Remove the skewers from heat and place them in a serving dish. Pour the reserved dressing over them and enjoy.

YIELD: 4 SERVINGS / **TOTAL TIME:** 2 HOURS

- 2 LARGE BEETS
- PINCH OF KOSHER SALT
- 2 TABLESPOONS CHOPPED WALNUTS
- 2 TABLESPOONS CHOPPED HAZELNUTS
- 2 TABLESPOONS CHOPPED PISTACHIOS
- 2 TEASPOONS BLACK PEPPER
- 2 TEASPOONS POPPY SEEDS
- 2 TEASPOONS BLACK SESAME SEEDS
- FULL-FAT GREEK YOGURT, FOR SERVING
- 1 CINNAMON STICK

GRILLED BEETS
WITH DUKKAH

1. Place the beets and salt in a saucepan with at least 5 cups of water and bring to a boil. Cook the beets until a knife can easily pass through them, 30 to 40 minutes.

2. Drain the beets, run them under cold water, and peel off the skins and stems; it is easiest to do this while the beets are still hot.

3. Cut the peeled beets into ¾-inch cubes and set them aside.

4. Prepare a gas or charcoal grill, setting up one zone for direct heat and another for indirect.

5. Place the nuts in a resealable bag and use a rolling pin to crush them. Transfer them to a small bowl, add the black pepper and seeds, and stir to combine. Set the dukkah aside.

6. Place your hand over the grate to test the heat in each section. Place the beets over high heat—a spot you can only leave your hand over for 2 seconds before you need to move it away. Cook until the beets are lightly charred all over, about 5 minutes, turning them as necessary.

7. Remove the beets from heat. To serve, spread the yogurt across a shallow bowl, pile the beets on top, and sprinkle the dukkah over the dish. Grate the cinnamon stick over the beets until the dish is to your taste and enjoy.

APPETIZERS, SIDES & SALADS

YIELD: 2 SERVINGS / **TOTAL TIME:** 30 MINUTES

1 CUP CHAMPAGNE VINEGAR OR WHITE WINE VINEGAR

½ CUP FRESH ORANGE JUICE

3 TABLESPOONS SUGAR, PLUS MORE AS NEEDED

½ TEASPOON KOSHER SALT, PLUS MORE TO TASTE

½ BULB OF FENNEL, TRIMMED AND SHAVED THIN

2 TABLESPOONS MINCED FRESH GINGER

½ CUP GREEK YOGURT

3 RIPE PLUMS, HALVED AND PITTED

FENNEL PESTO (SEE PAGE 217)

1 CARA CARA ORANGE, PEELED AND SLICED, FOR GARNISH

CARAMELIZED PLUMS
WITH FENNEL, ORANGE, GINGER YOGURT & PINE NUTS

1. Place the vinegar, orange juice, sugar, and salt in a small saucepan and bring to a boil. Place the shaved fennel in a mason jar and pour the hot brine over it. Cover the jar with plastic wrap and let the fennel pickle.

2. Place the ginger and yogurt in a bowl and stir to combine. Set the mixture aside.

3. Prepare a gas or charcoal grill, setting up one zone for direct heat and another for indirect.

4. Place sugar in a shallow bowl and coat the cut sides of the plums with it. Place your hand over the grate to test the heat in each section. Place the plums over medium heat—a spot you can leave your hand over for 5 seconds before you need to move it away—with the cut sides facing down. Cook until they are caramelized, 3 to 5 minutes.

5. Remove the plums from the grill, chop them, and season with salt. Place them in a bowl, add the pickled fennel, and toss to combine.

6. Spread the yogurt mixture over the bottom of a serving dish. Arrange the plums and pickled fennel on top, drizzle the Fennel Pesto over the salad, garnish with the orange, and serve.

APPETIZERS, SIDES & SALADS

YIELD: 6 SERVINGS / **TOTAL TIME:** 1 HOUR AND 15 MINUTES

6 EARS OF CORN, UNSHUCKED

3 CHIPOTLE CHILE PEPPERS IN ADOBO

½ CUP MAYONNAISE

¼ CUP SOUR CREAM

1½ TABLESPOONS BROWN SUGAR

1 TABLESPOON FRESH LIME JUICE

2 TABLESPOONS CHOPPED CILANTRO, PLUS MORE FOR GARNISH

1 TEASPOON KOSHER SALT, PLUS MORE TO TASTE

½ TEASPOON BLACK PEPPER, PLUS MORE TO TASTE

3 TABLESPOONS EXTRA-VIRGIN OLIVE OIL

½ CUP CRUMBLED GOAT CHEESE

LIME WEDGES, FOR SERVING

ELOTES

1. Prepare a gas or charcoal grill, setting up one zone for direct heat and another for indirect.

2. Place your hand over the grate to test the heat in each section. Place the corn over medium-low heat—a spot you can leave your hand over for 6 or 7 seconds before you need to move it away. Cook until the kernels have a slight give to them, about 25 minutes.

3. Remove the corn from heat and let it cool. When the corn is cool enough to handle, shuck it.

4. Place the chipotles, mayonnaise, sour cream, brown sugar, lime juice, cilantro, salt, and pepper in a food processor and blitz until smooth. Set the mixture aside.

5. Drizzle the olive oil over the corn and season it with salt and pepper. Place the corn over medium-high heat—a spot you can leave your hand over for 3 or 4 seconds before you need to move it away. Cook until the corn is charred all over, about 5 minutes, turning it as necessary.

6. Remove the corn from heat and spread the mayonnaise mixture over it. Sprinkle the goat cheese over the top, garnish with additional cilantro, and serve with lime wedges.

YIELD: 4 SERVINGS / **TOTAL TIME:** 35 MINUTES

1 LARGE HEAD OF GREEN CABBAGE

2 TABLESPOONS EXTRA-VIRGIN OLIVE OIL

1½ TEASPOONS GARLIC POWDER

SALT AND PEPPER, TO TASTE

GRILLED CABBAGE

1. Prepare a gas or charcoal grill, setting up one zone for direct heat and another for indirect.

2. Cut the head of cabbage into 8 wedges. Remove the core, brush the wedges with the olive oil, and season them with the garlic powder, salt, and pepper.

3. Place your hand over the grate to test the heat in each section. Place the cabbage over medium-high heat—a spot you can leave your hand over for 3 or 4 seconds before you need to move it away. Cook the cabbage until it is charred and tender, about 10 minutes, trying to turn it as little as possible.

4. Remove the cabbage from the grill and serve immediately.

YIELD: 2 TO 4 SERVINGS / **TOTAL TIME:** 50 MINUTES

4 CUPS EXTRA-VIRGIN OLIVE OIL

4 SPRIGS OF FRESH THYME

3 GARLIC CLOVES, CRUSHED

1 SPRIG OF FRESH SAGE, PLUS MORE, CHOPPED, FOR GARNISH

3 DELICATA SQUASH, SEEDED AND SLICED INTO RINGS

SALT AND PEPPER, TO TASTE

APPLE SLICES, FOR GARNISH

SPICED PEPITAS (SEE PAGE 209), FOR GARNISH

1 CUP APPLE BUTTER (SEE PAGE 212), FOR SERVING

POACHED & GRILLED
DELICATA SQUASH

1. Preheat the oven to 325°F. Place the olive oil, thyme, garlic, and sage in a saucepan and warm the mixture over low heat.

2. Place the squash in a deep baking dish and pour the olive oil and herbs over it. Place the squash in the oven and roast until it is fork-tender, about 15 minutes. Remove the squash from the oven and set it aside. Reserve the olive oil..

3. Prepare a gas or charcoal grill, setting up one zone for direct heat and another for indirect.

4. Place your hand over the grate to test the heat in each section and place the squash over medium-high heat—a spot you can leave your hand over for 3 to 4 seconds before you need to move it away. Cook until it is lightly charred on both sides, turning it over just once.

5. Remove the squash from the grill, place it on a plate, and tent it with aluminum foil to keep warm.

6. Place some of the reserved olive oil in a skillet and warm it over high heat. Add some chopped sage and fry it for 1 minute.

7. Transfer the squash to a serving dish, garnish with sliced apples, the Spiced Pepitas, and fried sage, and serve with the Apple Butter.

APPETIZERS, SIDES & SALADS

POACHED & GRILLED DELICATA SQUASH

See page 155

YIELD: 4 SERVINGS / **TOTAL TIME:** 1 HOUR

1 TABLESPOON DIJON MUSTARD

¼ CUP PLUS 1 TABLESPOON EXTRA-VIRGIN OLIVE OIL

3 TABLESPOONS BALSAMIC VINEGAR

3 TABLESPOONS RED WINE VINEGAR

1 LB. YELLOW SQUASH, SLICED LENGTHWISE

1 LARGE ZUCCHINI, SLICED LENGTHWISE

3 CUPS BABY SPINACH

½ CUP CHERRY TOMATOES, HALVED

6 FRESH BASIL LEAVES, CHOPPED

3 FRESH MINT LEAVES, CHOPPED

⅓ CUP FETA CHEESE, CRUMBLED

SUMMER SQUASH SALAD

1. Place the Dijon mustard, ¼ cup of olive oil, the balsamic vinegar, and red wine vinegar in a bowl and whisk until well combined. Set the dressing aside.

2. Place the squash and zucchini in a bowl, add the remaining olive oil, and toss to coat. Set the squash and zucchini aside.

3. Prepare a gas or charcoal grill, setting up one zone for direct heat and another for indirect.

4. Place your hand over the grate to test the heat in each section. Place the squash and zucchini over medium-high heat—a spot you can leave your hand over for 3 or 4 seconds before you need to move it away. Cook until the vegetables are charred and tender, 6 to 8 minutes, turning them over just once.

5. Remove the squash and zucchini from heat and cut them into bite-size pieces. Place them in a salad bowl, add the spinach, cherry tomatoes, basil, mint, and dressing, and toss to coat.

6. Top the salad with the feta and enjoy.

YIELD: 4 SERVINGS / **TOTAL TIME:** 30 MINUTES

HANDFUL OF BAY LEAVES

12 OYSTERS, RINSED AND SCRUBBED

7 TABLESPOONS EXTRA-VIRGIN OLIVE OIL

7 TABLESPOONS FRESH LIME JUICE

1 CUP CHOPPED FRESH CILANTRO

GRILLED OYSTERS

1. Prepare a gas or charcoal grill, setting up one zone for direct heat and another for indirect.

2. Distribute the bay leaves over the coals and set up a grate over them.

3. Place your hand over the grate to test the heat in each section. Place the oysters over medium-high heat—a spot you can leave your hand over for 3 or 4 seconds before you need to move it away. Cook until they start

to open and absorb the smoke. Using tongs, carefully remove the oysters and arrange them on a platter or serving board. Discard any oysters that did not open.

4. Place the olive oil, lime juice, and cilantro in a bowl and stir until thoroughly combined. Serve this sauce alongside the oysters.

GRILLED OYSTERS
See page 159

YIELD: 4 SERVINGS / **TOTAL TIME:** 1 HOUR

1 ONION, QUARTERED

1 LARGE EGGPLANT, TRIMMED AND HALVED LENGTHWISE

1 RED BELL PEPPER

2 TEASPOONS KOSHER SALT

¼ CUP AVOCADO OIL

¼ CUP BALSAMIC VINEGAR

CHARRED EGGPLANT

1. Prepare a gas or charcoal grill, setting up one zone for direct heat and another for indirect.

2. Place your hand over the grate to test the heat in each section. Place the onion, eggplant, and peppers over medium heat—a spot you can leave your hand over for 5 seconds before you need to move it away. Cook until the onion and pepper are tender and lightly charred, and the eggplant is charred and has collapsed. This will take 15 to 20 minutes for the onion and pepper and 25 to 30 minutes for the eggplant.

3. Remove the vegetables from heat. Place the pepper in a bowl and cover it with aluminum foil. Let it steam for 5 minutes. Chop the eggplant and place it in a bowl. Place the onion in a food processor and blitz until it is pureed. Spread the puree over a serving dish.

4. Remove the pepper from the bowl and chop it into bite-size pieces. Add it to the bowl containing the eggplant along with the salt, avocado oil, and balsamic vinegar. Toss to coat, pile the mixture on top of the onion puree, and enjoy.

YIELD: 4 SERVINGS / **TOTAL TIME:** 1 HOUR

2 BELL PEPPERS

2 RED ONIONS, HALVED

SALT, TO TASTE

EXTRA-VIRGIN OLIVE OIL, TO TASTE

FIRE-ROASTED PEPPERS & ONIONS

1. Prepare a gas or charcoal grill, setting up one zone for direct heat and another for indirect.

2. Place your hand over the grate to test the heat in each section. Place the peppers and onions over low heat—a spot you can comfortably leave your hand over for 9 seconds. Roast the vegetables until they are tender and charred all over, about 40 minutes for the onions and 25 minutes for the peppers. Turn the vegetables as little as necessary as they roast.

3. Transfer the peppers to a metal mixing bowl, cover the bowl with plastic wrap, and let them steam for 10 minutes. Place the onions on a cutting board and let them cool slightly.

4. Peel the peppers and remove the stems and seed pods. Chop the peppers and place them in a bowl. When the onions are cool enough to handle, chop them and add them to the bowl.

5. Season the mixture with salt and drizzle a generous amount of olive oil over the top. Toss to combine and enjoy.

YIELD: 4 SERVINGS / **TOTAL TIME:** 35 MINUTES

1 BUNCH OF ASPARAGUS, TRIMMED

3 TABLESPOONS EXTRA-VIRGIN OLIVE OIL

½ TEASPOON KOSHER SALT

½ TEASPOON BLACK PEPPER

2 LEMON WEDGES

GRILLED ASPARAGUS

1. Prepare a gas or charcoal grill, setting up one zone for direct heat and another for indirect.

2. Place the asparagus in a baking dish, drizzle the olive oil over the top, and season it with the salt and pepper. Toss to coat.

3. Place your hand over the grate to test the heat in each section. Place the asparagus over medium heat—a spot you can leave your hand over for 5 seconds before you need to move it away. Cook until the asparagus is browned and tender, about 10 minutes, turning it as necessary.

4. Remove the asparagus from heat, squeeze the juice of the lemon wedges over it, and enjoy.

YIELD: 4 SERVINGS / **TOTAL TIME:** 30 MINUTES

4 LEEKS, TRIMMED, RINSED WELL, AND HALVED LENGTHWISE

2 TABLESPOONS EXTRA-VIRGIN OLIVE OIL

SALT AND PEPPER, TO TASTE

ROMESCO SAUCE (SEE PAGE 198), FOR SERVING

GRILLED LEEKS
WITH ROMESCO

1. Prepare a gas or charcoal grill, setting up one zone for direct heat and another for indirect.

2. Place your hand over the grate to test the heat in each section. Place the leeks, cut side down, over medium-high heat—a spot you can leave your hand over for 3 or 4 seconds before you need to move it away. Cook until the leeks are charred on both sides and tender, 8 to 12 minutes, turning them over just once.

3. Remove the leeks from the grill, chop them, and place them in a serving dish. Drizzle the olive oil over the leeks, season them with salt and pepper, and serve alongside the Romesco Sauce.

YIELD: 2 SERVINGS / **TOTAL TIME:** 45 MINUTES

CANOLA OIL, AS NEEDED

1 CUP SHREDDED BAKED SWEET POTATO SKINS

1 TABLESPOON KOSHER SALT

2 TEASPOONS BLACK PEPPER

½ GREEN APPLE

½ CUP WHITE VINEGAR

1 HEART OF ROMAINE LETTUCE

2 TEASPOONS EXTRA-VIRGIN OLIVE OIL

1 TABLESPOON BALSAMIC VINEGAR

2 TABLESPOONS CRUMBLED FETA CHEESE

GRILLED ROMAINE
& CRISPY SWEET POTATO

1. Add canola oil to a small saucepan until it is about 2 inches deep and warm it to 350°F. Add the sweet potato skins and fry until golden brown and crispy, about 1 minute. Remove the fried sweet potato skins from the oil and place them on a paper towel–lined plate. Season the potato skins with 1 teaspoon of the salt and 1 teaspoon of the pepper.

2. Prepare a gas or charcoal grill, setting up one zone for direct heat and another for indirect.

3. Cut the apple into ½-inch-thick slices, leaving the skin on. Place the apple in a small bowl, add the white vinegar and 1 teaspoon of the salt, and toss to coat. Set the mixture aside.

4. Cut off the stem from the heart of romaine, separate the leaves, and place them in a bowl. Add the olive oil, remaining salt, and remaining pepper and toss to coat.

5. Place your hand over the grate to test the heat in each section. Place the romaine lettuce over high heat—a spot you can only leave your hand over for 2 seconds before you need to move it away. Cook the lettuce until it is slightly charred on both sides, but before it starts to wilt, about 1 minute.

6. Arrange the lettuce on a plate, crumble the fried sweet potato skins over them, and distribute the apple on top. Drizzle the balsamic over the dish, sprinkle the feta on top, and enjoy.

YIELD: 6 SERVINGS / **TOTAL TIME:** 24 HOURS

4 LBS. TURKEY WINGS, SEPARATED INTO DRUMETTES AND FLATS

¼ CUP HOT SAUCE, PLUS MORE TO TASTE

3 TABLESPOONS EXTRA-VIRGIN OLIVE OIL

SALT, TO TASTE

4 TABLESPOONS UNSALTED BUTTER, MELTED

SPICY TURKEY WINGS

1. Pat the wings dry with paper towels. Place the wings in a resealable plastic bag and add the hot sauce, olive oil, and salt. Toss to coat the wings and let them marinate in the refrigerator overnight.

2. Prepare a gas or charcoal grill, setting up one zone for direct heat and another for indirect.

3. Place your hand over the grate to test the heat in each section. Place the wings over medium-low heat—a spot you can leave your hand over for 6 or 7 seconds before you need to move it away. Cook for 20 minutes.

4. Turn the wings over and cook until they are cooked through and crispy, about 8 minutes.

5. Remove the wings from the grill, place them in a bowl, and add the butter and additional hot sauce. Toss to coat and enjoy.

YIELD: 8 SERVINGS / **TOTAL TIME:** 40 MINUTES

1 LINK OF CHORIZO, CASING REMOVED

14 BUTTON MUSHROOMS, STEMMED

6 TABLESPOONS EXTRA-VIRGIN OLIVE OIL

1 ONION, FINELY DICED

4 CHERRY TOMATOES, MINCED

1 TEASPOON FRESH THYME

¼ CUP CHICKEN STOCK (SEE PAGE 215)

1 SMALL BUNCH OF FRESH PARSLEY, CHOPPED

¼ CUP GRATED PARMESAN CHEESE

SALT AND PEPPER, TO TASTE

CHORIZO-STUFFED MUSHROOMS

1. Prepare a gas or charcoal grill, setting up one zone for direct heat and another for indirect.

2. Place the chorizo in a food processor and blitz until it is a thick paste. Set the chorizo aside.

3. Brush the mushroom caps with 2 tablespoons of olive oil. Place your hand over the grate to test the heat in each section. Place the mushroom caps over medium-high heat—a spot you can leave your hand over for 3 or 4 seconds before you need to move it away. Cook until the tops have browned, about 2 minutes. Remove the mushroom caps from the grill and set them aside.

4. Place the remaining olive oil in a cast-iron skillet and place it over medium-high heat. Add the onion, cherry tomatoes, and thyme and cook, stirring occasionally, until the onion is translucent, about 3 minutes.

5. Stir in the chorizo and cook until it is browned, about 7 minutes. Add the stock and parsley and cook for another minute. Remove the pan from heat.

6. Stuff the mushroom caps with the chorizo mixture and place them in a clean cast-iron skillet. Sprinkle some Parmesan over each stuffed mushroom and place the pan over medium-low heat—a spot you can leave your hand over for 6 or 7 seconds before you need to move it away. Cook until the mushrooms are cooked through, about 10 minutes.

7. Remove the pan from heat, season the stuffed mushrooms with salt and pepper, and enjoy.

APPETIZERS, SIDES & SALADS

YIELD: 4 SERVINGS / **TOTAL TIME:** 45 MINUTES

2 LBS. CHICKEN THIGHS, GROUND

1 LARGE EGG, LIGHTLY BEATEN

1 CUP PANKO

2 TEASPOONS MISO PASTE

2 TABLESPOONS SAKE

1½ TABLESPOONS MIRIN

½ TEASPOON BLACK PEPPER

SESAME SEEDS, FOR GARNISH

2 SCALLIONS, TRIMMED AND SLICED, FOR GARNISH

TARE SAUCE (SEE PAGE 216), FOR SERVING

CHICKEN TSUKUNE

1. Place the ground chicken, egg, bread crumbs, miso, sake, mirin, and pepper in a bowl and stir to combine. Cover the bowl and place it in the refrigerator while you prepare a fire.

2. Prepare a gas or charcoal grill, setting up one zone for direct heat and another for indirect.

3. Remove the chicken mixture from the refrigerator, form it into balls or ovals, and thread the meatballs onto skewers.

4. Place your hand over the grate to test the heat in each section. Place the meatballs over medium-high heat—a spot you can leave your hand over for 3 or 4 seconds before you need to move it away. Cook until they are browned all over and cooked through, 6 to 8 minutes, turning them as necessary.

5. Remove the meatballs from heat, garnish them with sesame seeds and the scallions, and serve with the Tare Sauce.

LICENSE TO GRILL

RUBS, MARINADES & SAUCES

Once you learn to master the flame, you'll want to expand your repertoire and experiment with new flavors. These recipes help you do just that, providing an easy path to exceptional results.

SWEET & SPICY RUB

YIELD: ½ CUP / **TOTAL TIME:** 5 MINUTES

⅓ CUP LIGHT BROWN SUGAR

1 TEASPOON CAYENNE PEPPER

1 TEASPOON CHILI POWDER

1½ TEASPOONS PAPRIKA

2 TEASPOONS FINE SEA SALT

1 TEASPOON GARLIC POWDER

1 TEASPOON ONION POWDER

1 TEASPOON CUMIN

1 TEASPOON BLACK PEPPER

½ TEASPOON MUSTARD POWDER

¼ TEASPOON DRIED OREGANO

Place all of the ingredients in a bowl, stir to combine, and use immediately or store in an airtight container.

ACAPULCO GOLD RUB

YIELD: 4 CUPS / **TOTAL TIME:** 5 MINUTES

1 CUP BROWN SUGAR

½ CUP KOSHER SALT

½ CUP CHILI POWDER

¼ CUP HUNGARIAN PAPRIKA

¼ CUP CORIANDER

1 TABLESPOON GROUND GINGER

¼ CUP CUMIN

⅓ CUP GARLIC POWDER

⅓ CUP ONION POWDER

1 TABLESPOON LEMON ZEST

¼ CUP DUTCH COCOA POWDER

Place all of the ingredients in a bowl, stir to combine, and use immediately or store in an airtight container.

MOLE RUB

YIELD: ¼ CUP / **TOTAL TIME:** 5 MINUTES

1 TABLESPOON ALLSPICE

1½ TEASPOONS GROUND CLOVES

1½ TEASPOONS CINNAMON

1½ TEASPOONS CUMIN

1 TABLESPOON CORIANDER

1 TABLESPOON GROUND GINGER

Place all of the ingredients in a small bowl, stir to combine, and use immediately or store in an airtight container.

LEMON & HERB POULTRY RUB

YIELD: 1½ CUPS / **TOTAL TIME:** 5 MINUTES

1 CUP SUGAR

2 TABLESPOONS KOSHER SALT

2 TEASPOONS BLACK PEPPER

2 TEASPOONS LEMON ZEST

1 TABLESPOON CHOPPED FRESH ROSEMARY

1 TABLESPOON FRESH THYME

1 TABLESPOON CHOPPED FRESH PARSLEY

Place all of the ingredients in a bowl, stir to combine, and use immediately or store in an airtight container.

BRISKET RUB

YIELD: 1¼ CUPS / **TOTAL TIME:** 5 MINUTES

½ CUP PAPRIKA

6 TABLESPOONS BLACK PEPPER

2 TABLESPOONS CHIPOTLE CHILE POWDER

2 TABLESPOONS CHILI POWDER

4 TEASPOONS CAYENNE PEPPER

2 TEASPOONS CUMIN

2 TEASPOONS DRIED OREGANO

1 TABLESPOON KOSHER SALT

Place all of the ingredients in a bowl, stir to combine, and use immediately or store in an airtight container.

RUSTIC STEAK RUB

YIELD: ½ CUP / **TOTAL TIME:** 5 MINUTES

6 GARLIC CLOVES, MINCED

2 TABLESPOONS THYME

2 TABLESPOONS KOSHER SALT

1½ TABLESPOONS BLACK PEPPER

1½ TABLESPOONS WHITE PEPPER

1 TABLESPOON RED PEPPER FLAKES

1 TABLESPOON SWEET PAPRIKA

1½ TEASPOONS ONION POWDER

Place all of the ingredients in a bowl, stir to combine, and use immediately or store in an airtight container.

SMOKED PAPRIKA RUB

YIELD: ¾ CUP / **TOTAL TIME:** 5 MINUTES

¼ CUP SMOKED PAPRIKA

4 TEASPOONS CORIANDER

4 TEASPOONS CUMIN

2 TEASPOONS CAYENNE PEPPER

2 TABLESPOONS BLACK PEPPER

2 TABLESPOONS KOSHER SALT

Place all of the ingredients in a bowl, stir to combine, and use immediately or store in an airtight container.

SEAFOOD RUB

YIELD: 1 CUP / **TOTAL TIME:** 5 MINUTES

1½ TABLESPOONS KOSHER SALT

3 TABLESPOONS PAPRIKA

3 TABLESPOONS ONION POWDER

3 TABLESPOONS BLACK PEPPER

1 TABLESPOONS CAJUN SEASONING

3 TABLESPOONS TURMERIC

3 TABLESPOONS CORIANDER

Place all of the ingredients in a bowl, stir to combine, and use immediately or store in an airtight container.

BRISKET RUB
See page 176

CHILE RUB

YIELD: ¾ CUP / **TOTAL TIME:** 5 MINUTES

½ CUP ANCHO CHILE POWDER

1 TABLESPOON PAPRIKA

1 TABLESPOON BLACK PEPPER

1 TABLESPOON KOSHER SALT

2 TEASPOONS CUMIN

1 TEASPOON CAYENNE PEPPER

1 TEASPOON MUSTARD POWDER

1 TEASPOON DRIED OREGANO

Place all of the ingredients in a bowl, stir to combine, and use immediately or store in an airtight container.

KASHMIRI CHILE RUB

YIELD: ½ CUP / **TOTAL TIME:** 5 MINUTES

3 TABLESPOONS KASHMIRI CHILE POWDER

3 TABLESPOONS SMOKED PAPRIKA

1 TABLESPOON DRIED OREGANO

2 TEASPOONS CUMIN

2 TEASPOONS BLACK PEPPER

2 TEASPOONS FINE SEA SALT

1 TEASPOON DRIED THYME

Place all of the ingredients in a bowl, stir to combine, and use immediately or store in an airtight container.

SMOKY ST. LOUIS RUB

YIELD: ¾ CUP / **TOTAL TIME:** 5 MINUTES

¼ CUP PAPRIKA

3 TABLESPOONS GARLIC POWDER

2 TABLESPOONS BLACK PEPPER

2 TABLESPOONS KOSHER SALT

2 TABLESPOONS ONION POWDER

1 TABLESPOON DARK BROWN SUGAR

1 TABLESPOON GROUND GINGER

1 TABLESPOON MUSTARD POWDER

2 TEASPOONS LIQUID SMOKE

1 TEASPOON CELERY SALT

Place all of the ingredients in a bowl, stir to combine, and use immediately or store in an airtight container.

FIVE-ALARM RUB

YIELD: ½ CUP / **TOTAL TIME:** 5 MINUTES

½ HABANERO CHILE PEPPER, STEM AND SEEDS REMOVED, MINCED

1 TABLESPOON GROUND STAR ANISE

1 TABLESPOON CINNAMON

1 TABLESPOON GROUND SICHUAN PEPPER

1 TABLESPOON GROUND FENNEL SEEDS

1 TABLESPOON GROUND CLOVES

1 TABLESPOON GARLIC POWDER

1 TABLESPOON GROUND GINGER

1 TABLESPOON FINE SEA SALT

Place all of the ingredients in a bowl, stir to combine, and use immediately or store in an airtight container.

SPICY SOUTHWESTERN RUB

YIELD: ½ CUP / **TOTAL TIME:** 5 MINUTES

2 TABLESPOONS CHILI POWDER

2 TABLESPOONS PAPRIKA

1 TABLESPOON CAYENNE PEPPER

1 TABLESPOON CUMIN

1 TABLESPOON MINCED HABANERO CHILE PEPPER

1 TABLESPOON CORIANDER

1 TABLESPOON GRATED GARLIC

1 TABLESPOON KOSHER SALT

1 TABLESPOON BLACK PEPPER

Place all of the ingredients in a mixing bowl, stir to combine, and use immediately or store in an air-tight container.

BLACKENING SPICE

YIELD: ¼ CUP / **TOTAL TIME:** 5 MINUTES

1½ TABLESPOONS PAPRIKA

1 TABLESPOON CHILI POWDER

1 TABLESPOON CUMIN

1½ TEASPOONS CORIANDER

½ TEASPOON CAYENNE PEPPER

1 TABLESPOON ONION POWDER

2 TEASPOONS GARLIC POWDER

2 TEASPOONS BLACK PEPPER

Place all of the ingredients in a mixing bowl, stir to combine, and use immediately or store in an air-tight container.

ZA'ATAR

YIELD: 1½ CUPS / **TOTAL TIME:** 5 MINUTES

1 TABLESPOON CUMIN

1 TABLESPOON SUMAC

1 TABLESPOON THYME

2 TEASPOONS HEMP SEEDS

2 TEASPOONS CRUSHED, TOASTED SUNFLOWER SEEDS

2 TABLESPOONS SESAME SEEDS

2 TABLESPOONS KOSHER SALT

1 TABLESPOON BLACK PEPPER

2 TABLESPOONS CHOPPED FRESH OREGANO

2 TABLESPOONS CHOPPED FRESH BASIL

2 TABLESPOONS CHOPPED FRESH PARSLEY

1 TABLESPOON GARLIC POWDER

1 TABLESPOON ONION POWDER

Place all of the ingredients in a bowl, stir to combine, and use immediately or store in an airtight container.

CAJUN RUB

YIELD: ½ CUP / **TOTAL TIME:** 5 MINUTES

¼ CUP FINE SEA SALT

2 TEASPOONS LIQUID SMOKE

2 TABLESPOONS BLACK PEPPER

2 TEASPOONS SMOKED PAPRIKA

2 TEASPOONS GARLIC POWDER

1 TEASPOON ONION POWDER

1 TEASPOON CAYENNE PEPPER

1 TEASPOON DRIED THYME

Place all of the ingredients in a bowl, stir to combine, and use immediately or store in an airtight container.

CAJUN RUB
See page 183

BBQ POULTRY RUB

YIELD: 1½ CUPS / **TOTAL TIME:** 5 MINUTES

⅓ CUP KOSHER SALT

½ CUP BROWN SUGAR

¼ CUP SMOKED PAPRIKA

1 TABLESPOON CAYENNE PEPPER

1 TABLESPOON CHILI POWDER

2 TEASPOONS CUMIN

1 TABLESPOON ONION POWDER

2 TABLESPOONS GARLIC POWDER

1 TABLESPOON BLACK PEPPER

1 TABLESPOON GROUND FENNEL SEEDS

1 TABLESPOON CORIANDER

1 TABLESPOON DRY MUSTARD

Place all of the ingredients in a bowl, stir to combine, and use immediately or store in an airtight container.

JERK SPICE RUB

YIELD: 1¾ CUPS / **TOTAL TIME:** 5 MINUTES

1 TABLESPOON ONION POWDER

1 TABLESPOON GARLIC POWDER

1 TABLESPOON DRIED THYME

1 TABLESPOON ADOBO SEASONING

2 TEASPOONS SAZÓN

2 TEASPOONS CAYENNE PEPPER

2 TEASPOONS KOSHER SALT

2 TEASPOONS BLACK PEPPER

1 TABLESPOON ALLSPICE

1 TABLESPOON PAPRIKA

1 TEASPOON RED PEPPER FLAKES

1 TEASPOON CUMIN

2 TEASPOONS CINNAMON

½ TEASPOON NUTMEG

1 TEASPOON GROUND CLOVES

1 TEASPOON GROUND GINGER

1 CUP EPIS (SEE PAGE 193)

1 TABLESPOON BROWNING SAUCE

Place all of the ingredients in a mixing bowl, stir to combine, and use immediately or store in an air-tight container.

POULTRY BRINE

YIELD: 18 CUPS / **TOTAL TIME:** 5 MINUTES

16 CUPS WARM WATER

1 CUP FINE SEA SALT

1 CUP LIGHT BROWN SUGAR

¼ CUP EXTRA-VIRGIN OLIVE OIL

JUICE OF ½ LEMON

4 GARLIC CLOVES, CRUSHED

1 TABLESPOON BLACK PEPPER

Place all of the ingredients in a stockpot and stir to combine. Use immediately or cover until ready to use.

JERK MARINADE

YIELD: 1½ CUPS / **TOTAL TIME:** 5 MINUTES

1 MEDIUM ONION, FINELY DICED

¼ CUP SCALLIONS, TRIMMED AND FINELY DICED

1 SCOTCH BONNET PEPPER, CHOPPED

3 TABLESPOONS SOY SAUCE

1 TABLESPOON WHITE VINEGAR

3 TABLESPOONS EXTRA-VIRGIN OLIVE OIL

2 TEASPOONS FRESH THYME

2 TEASPOONS SUGAR

1 TEASPOON FINE SEA SALT

1 TEASPOON BLACK PEPPER

1 TEASPOON ALLSPICE

½ TEASPOON FRESHLY GRATED NUTMEG

½ TEASPOON CINNAMON

Place all of the ingredients in a food processor, blitz until smooth, and use immediately or store in an airtight container.

RED WINE & HERB MARINADE

YIELD: 2½ CUPS / **TOTAL TIME:** 5 MINUTES

2 CUPS RED WINE

2 TABLESPOONS RED WINE VINEGAR

2 GARLIC CLOVES, MINCED

1 TEASPOON FRESH THYME

1 TABLESPOON CHOPPED FRESH ROSEMARY

½ SMALL WHITE ONION, FINELY DICED

1 TEASPOON FRESH LEMON JUICE

½ TEASPOON DRIED OREGANO

1 TEASPOON BLACK PEPPER

1 TEASPOON FINE SEA SALT

Place all of the ingredients in a bowl, whisk to combine, and use immediately or store in an airtight container.

LAMB MARINADE

YIELD: 1½ CUPS / **TOTAL TIME:** 5 MINUTES

8 GARLIC CLOVES, MINCED

1 TABLESPOON CUMIN

2 TABLESPOONS BLACK PEPPER

1 TABLESPOON GROUND FENNEL

1 TABLESPOON PAPRIKA

2 TABLESPOONS KOSHER SALT

2 TEASPOONS DIJON MUSTARD

1 CUP EXTRA-VIRGIN OLIVE OIL

Place all of the ingredients in a bowl, stir to combine, and use immediately or store in an airtight container.

CITRUS & SAGE MARINADE

YIELD: 1 CUP / **TOTAL TIME:** 5 MINUTES

3 GARLIC CLOVES

⅓ CUP FRESH SAGE

ZEST AND JUICE OF 1 ORANGE

1 TABLESPOON CORIANDER

1½ TEASPOONS BLACK PEPPER

½ TEASPOON RED PEPPER FLAKES

¼ CUP EXTRA-VIRGIN OLIVE OIL

Place all of the ingredients in a food processor, blitz until combined, and use immediately or store in an airtight container.

BAY BLEND MARINADE

YIELD: 1½ CUPS / **TOTAL TIME:** 5 MINUTES

12 BAY LEAVES

1 ONION, CHOPPED

6 GARLIC CLOVES, CHOPPED

2 CELERY STALKS, CHOPPED

½ TEASPOON ALLSPICE

¼ TEASPOON CINNAMON

½ TEASPOON GROUND GINGER

2 TEASPOONS BLACK PEPPER

1 TABLESPOON KOSHER SALT

¼ CUP EXTRA-VIRGIN OLIVE OIL

Place all of the ingredients in a food processor, blitz until smooth, and use immediately or store in the refrigerator.

SESAME & HONEY MARINADE

YIELD: 1¾ CUPS / **TOTAL TIME:** 5 MINUTES

¾ CUP KECAP MANIS

½ CUP RICE VINEGAR

¼ CUP SESAME OIL

¼ CUP HONEY

1 TEASPOON CINNAMON

1 TEASPOON BLACK PEPPER

1 TEASPOON SESAME SEEDS

Place all of the ingredients in a bowl, whisk to combine, and use immediately or store in the refrigerator.

PERI-PERI MARINADE

YIELD: 1½ CUPS / **TOTAL TIME:** 20 MINUTES

1 TEASPOON CORIANDER SEEDS

2 DRIED CHILE PEPPERS, STEMMED AND SEEDED

1 TABLESPOON DRIED OREGANO

1 TABLESPOON SWEET PAPRIKA

PINCH OF CINNAMON

2 TEASPOONS WORCESTERSHIRE SAUCE

2 GARLIC CLOVES, MINCED

JUICE OF 1 LIME

1 TABLESPOON HONEY

2 TEASPOONS KOSHER SALT

5 TABLESPOONS BALSAMIC VINEGAR

1 TABLESPOON WATER

¼ CUP EXTRA-VIRGIN OLIVE OIL

HANDFUL OF FRESH CILANTRO, CHOPPED

Place the coriander seeds and chiles in a small, dry saucepan and toast them over medium heat for 1 minute, shaking the pan occasionally. Stir in the oregano, paprika, cinnamon, Worcestershire sauce, garlic, lime juice, honey, salt, balsamic vinegar, and water and bring the mixture to a simmer. Cook for about 10 minutes.

Transfer the mixture to a blender, add the olive oil and cilantro, and blitz until smooth. Let the marinade cool completely before using.

MOLE MANCHAMANTELES

YIELD: 4 TO 6 CUPS / **TOTAL TIME:** 2 HOURS AND 30 MINUTES

½ LB. PILONCILLO

1 CUP WATER

1 APPLE, PEELED, CORED, AND SLICED

1 PEAR, PEELED, CORED, AND SLICED

1 PEACH, HALVED, PITTED, AND SLICED

¾ CUP SESAME SEEDS

½ MEXICAN CINNAMON STICK

1¼ TABLESPOONS CORIANDER SEEDS

1½ TEASPOONS ALLSPICE BERRIES

1 TABLESPOON CUMIN SEEDS

2 STAR ANISE PODS

1 WHITE ONION, QUARTERED

5 GARLIC CLOVES, UNPEELED

7 TABLESPOONS LARD

6 ANCHO CHILE PEPPERS, STEMMED AND SEEDED

5 GUAJILLO CHILE PEPPERS, STEMMED AND SEEDED

2 CHIPOTLE MECO CHILE PEPPERS, STEMMED AND SEEDED

½ CUP GOLDEN RAISINS

1 RIPE PLANTAIN, PEELED AND SLICED

10½ OZ. ROMA TOMATOES, HALVED

CHICKEN STOCK (SEE PAGE 215), AS NEEDED

SALT, TO TASTE

Preheat the oven to 400°F. Place the piloncillo and water in a saucepan and bring to a boil, stirring to dissolve the piloncillo. Toss the apple, pear, and peach into the syrup, transfer the mixture to a baking dish, and place it in the oven. Roast until the fruits are caramelized, about 20 minutes.

Place the sesame seeds in a dry skillet and toast until they are lightly browned, shaking the pan frequently. Add the cinnamon stick, coriander seeds, allspice berries, cumin seeds, and star anise to the skillet and toast until fragrant, shaking the pan frequently. Grind the mixture into a fine powder with a mortar and pestle or a spice grinder.

Place the onion and garlic in the skillet and cook over medium heat until they are charred, about 10 minutes, turning occasionally. Remove them from the pan and let them cool. When cool enough to handle, peel the garlic cloves.

Place the lard in a Dutch oven and warm it over medium heat. Add the chiles and fry until pliable and fragrant. Remove the chiles and soak them in hot water for 20 minutes.

Place the raisins and plantain in the lard and fry until the raisins are puffy and the plantain has caramelized. Add all of the ingredients to the Dutch oven and cook for 1 to 2 hours, adding stock as needed.

Place the mixture in a blender and puree until smooth. Strain, season with salt, and use as desired.

EPIS

EPIS

YIELD: 1 CUP / **TOTAL TIME:** 5 MINUTES

8 SCALLIONS, TRIMMED

½ BUNCH OF FRESH PARSLEY

1½ OZ. GARLIC CLOVES, CHOPPED

¼ LARGE ONION, CHOPPED

1 TABLESPOON FRESH THYME

¼ RED BELL PEPPER

¼ GREEN BELL PEPPER

¼ YELLOW BELL PEPPER

¼ ORANGE BELL PEPPER

¼ HABANERO CHILE PEPPER

2 TABLESPOONS EXTRA-VIRGIN OLIVE OIL

JUICE OF ½ LIME

SALT, TO TASTE

Place all of the ingredients in a blender and pulse until the mixture is a coarse paste.

Taste, adjust the seasoning as necessary, and pulse until smooth.

Use immediately or store in the refrigerator.

RECADO ROJO

YIELD: 3 CUPS / **TOTAL TIME:** 20 MINUTES

3½ OZ. ACHIOTE PASTE

14 TABLESPOONS FRESH LIME JUICE

14 TABLESPOONS ORANGE JUICE

7 TABLESPOONS GRAPEFRUIT JUICE

1 TEASPOON DRIED OREGANO

1 TEASPOON DRIED MARJORAM

1 HABANERO CHILE PEPPER, STEMMED AND SEEDED

5 GARLIC CLOVES

1 CINNAMON STICK, GRATED

SALT, TO TASTE

Place the achiote paste and juices in a bowl and let the mixture sit for 15 minutes.

Place the mixture and the remaining ingredients in a blender and puree until smooth.

Taste, adjust the seasoning as necessary, and use as desired.

RECADO ROJO

See page 193

CHIMICHURRI SAUCE

YIELD: 2 CUPS / **TOTAL TIME:** 10 MINUTES

1 CUP FRESH PARSLEY

2 LARGE GARLIC CLOVES, SMASHED

1 TEASPOON DRIED THYME

¼ TEASPOON RED PEPPER FLAKES

½ CUP WATER

¼ CUP WHITE WINE VINEGAR

¼ CUP EXTRA-VIRGIN OLIVE OIL

1 TEASPOON FINE SEA SALT

⅛ TEASPOON BLACK PEPPER

Use a mortar and pestle or a food processor to combine the ingredients until the sauce has the desired texture. Use immediately or store in the refrigerator.

RED CHERMOULA SAUCE

YIELD: 1 CUP / **TOTAL TIME:** 10 MINUTES

PINCH OF SAFFRON THREADS

¼ CUP HARISSA

½ CUP EXTRA-VIRGIN OLIVE OIL

1 TABLESPOON CHOPPED PRESERVED LEMONS

2 TEASPOONS KOSHER SALT

1 TABLESPOON SMOKED PAPRIKA

1 TEASPOON CUMIN POWDER

2 TEASPOONS FRESH LEMON JUICE

2 TABLESPOONS CHOPPED FRESH CILANTRO

1 TABLESPOON CHOPPED FRESH PARSLEY

1 TABLESPOON SLICED FRESH CHIVES

Using a mortar and pestle or food processor, combine all of the ingredients, except for the herbs, until the desired consistency has been achieved.

Add the herbs and stir until well combined.

Taste the sauce, adjust the seasoning as necessary, and use immediately or store in the refrigerator.

RED CHERMOULA SAUCE

REMOULADE SAUCE

YIELD: 2 CUPS / **TOTAL TIME:** 5 MINUTES

1½ CUPS MAYONNAISE

½ CUP CREOLE MUSTARD

JUICE OF 2 LEMONS

3 TABLESPOONS SRIRACHA

3 TABLESPOONS SWEET RELISH

¾ TEASPOON KOSHER SALT

½ TEASPOON BLACK PEPPER

Place all of the ingredients in a bowl and whisk until thoroughly combined. Use immediately or store in the refrigerator.

ROMESCO SAUCE

YIELD: 1 CUP / **TOTAL TIME:** 5 MINUTES

2 LARGE ROASTED RED BELL PEPPERS

1 GARLIC CLOVE, SMASHED

½ CUP SLIVERED ALMONDS, TOASTED

¼ CUP TOMATO PUREE

2 TABLESPOONS FINELY CHOPPED FLAT-LEAF PARSLEY

2 TABLESPOONS SHERRY VINEGAR

1 TEASPOON SMOKED PAPRIKA

SALT AND PEPPER, TO TASTE

½ CUP EXTRA-VIRGIN OLIVE OIL

Place all of the ingredients, except for the olive oil, in a blender or food processor and pulse until the mixture is smooth.

Add the olive oil in a steady stream and blitz until emulsified. Season with salt and pepper and use immediately.

SMOKY SOUTHERN BBQ SAUCE

YIELD: 1½ CUPS / **TOTAL TIME:** 1 HOUR AND 30 MINUTES

1 CUP HICKORY WOOD CHIPS

2 GARLIC CLOVES, MINCED

1 WHITE ONION, MINCED

1 CUP CRUSHED TOMATOES, DRAINED

¼ CUP TOMATO PASTE

2 TABLESPOONS WHITE WINE VINEGAR

2 TABLESPOONS BALSAMIC VINEGAR

1 TABLESPOON DIJON MUSTARD

JUICE FROM 1 LIME

1-INCH PIECE OF FRESH GINGER, PEELED AND MINCED

1 HABANERO CHILE PEPPER, STEMMED, SEEDED, AND MINCED

1 TEASPOON SMOKED PAPRIKA

½ TEASPOON CINNAMON

2 DRIED CHIPOTLE CHILE PEPPERS, STEMMED, SEEDED, AND MINCED

SALT AND PEPPER, TO TASTE

Soak the woodchips in a bowl of water for 20 minutes.

Prepare a fire, either setting up an even coal bed if you are able to adjust the height of your grate easily, or banking the coals to set up one zone for direct heat and another for indirect. Set up a grate over the coals.

Place the garlic, onion, tomatoes, and tomato paste in a food processor and blitz until combined. Add the remaining ingredients and blitz until incorporated. Pour the sauce into a saucepan.

Drain the woodchips and spread them over the coals. Place your hand over the grate to test the heat in each section. Place the saucepan over medium heat—a spot you can leave your hand over for 5 seconds before you need to move it away—and bring the sauce to a boil. Let the sauce cook until it has reduced by about one-third, about 20 minutes.

Taste, adjust the seasoning as necessary, and use immediately or store in the refrigerator.

KANSAS CITY BBQ SAUCE

YIELD: 1½ CUPS / **TOTAL TIME:** 30 MINUTES

1 TABLESPOON EXTRA-VIRGIN OLIVE OIL

4 GARLIC CLOVES, MINCED

1 CUP KETCHUP

¼ CUP WATER

2 TABLESPOONS MOLASSES

2 TABLESPOONS DARK BROWN SUGAR

1 TABLESPOON APPLE CIDER VINEGAR

1 TABLESPOON WORCESTERSHIRE SAUCE

1 BAY LEAF

1 TEASPOON MUSTARD POWDER

1 TEASPOON CHILI POWDER

1 TEASPOON ONION POWDER

1 TEASPOON LIQUID SMOKE

1 TEASPOON BLACK PEPPER

1 TEASPOON KOSHER SALT

Place the olive oil in a saucepan and warm it over medium-high heat. Add the garlic and cook, stirring continually, for 1 minute.

Stir in the remaining ingredients and bring the sauce to a boil. Reduce the heat to medium and simmer until the sauce has reduced by one-third, about 20 minutes.

Remove the bay leaf and discard it. Taste, adjust the seasoning as necessary, and use immediately, or let the sauce cool and store in the refrigerator.

SOUTH CAROLINA BBQ SAUCE

YIELD: 2 CUPS / **TOTAL TIME:** 30 MINUTES

1 CUP YELLOW MUSTARD

½ CUP HONEY

½ CUP APPLE CIDER VINEGAR

2 TABLESPOONS KETCHUP

1 TABLESPOON LIGHT BROWN SUGAR

2 TEASPOONS WORCESTERSHIRE SAUCE

3 GARLIC CLOVES, MINCED

1 TEASPOON GROUND BLACK PEPPER

SALT, TO TASTE

Place all of the ingredients in a saucepan, stir to combine, and bring to a boil over medium-high heat. Reduce the heat to medium and cook until the sauce has reduced by one-third, about 20 minutes.

Taste, adjust the seasoning as necessary, and use immediately, or let the sauce cool and store in the refrigerator.

COFFEE & BOURBON BBQ SAUCE

YIELD: 2 CUPS / **TOTAL TIME:** 30 MINUTES

2 CUPS BREWED COFFEE

¼ CUP DARK BROWN SUGAR

¾ CUP BOURBON

3 TABLESPOONS MOLASSES

¼ CUP APPLE CIDER VINEGAR

2 TABLESPOONS WORCESTERSHIRE SAUCE

¼ CUP KETCHUP

1 TABLESPOON GRANULATED GARLIC

½ TABLESPOON BLACK PEPPER

1 TABLESPOON CORNSTARCH

Place all of the ingredients in a saucepan, stir to combine, and bring the sauce to a boil over medium-high heat. Reduce the heat to medium and simmer the sauce until it has reduced by one-third, about 20 minutes.

Taste, adjust the seasoning as necessary, and use immediately, or let the sauce cool and store in the refrigerator.

MOLASSES BBQ SAUCE

YIELD: 1½ CUPS / **TOTAL TIME:** 30 MINUTES

½ CUP KETCHUP

¼ CUP DARK BROWN SUGAR

2 TABLESPOONS GRANULATED SUGAR

2 TABLESPOONS DIJON MUSTARD

3 TABLESPOONS APPLE CIDER VINEGAR

2 GARLIC CLOVES, MINCED

¼ CUP BLACKSTRAP MOLASSES

¼ TEASPOON GROUND CLOVES

½ TEASPOON HOT SAUCE

¼ CUP HONEY

Place all of the ingredients in a medium saucepan and bring to a boil over medium-high heat. Reduce the heat so that the sauce simmers and cook, stirring occasionally, until the sauce has reduced by one-third, about 20 minutes.

Taste, adjust the seasoning as necessary, and use immediately, or let the sauce cool and store in the refrigerator.

COFFEE & BOURBON BBQ SAUCE

See page 201

SALSA MACHA

PICO DE GALLO

YIELD: 1 CUP / **TOTAL TIME:** 25 MINUTES

2 LARGE TOMATOES, FINELY DICED

½ ONION, FINELY DICED

2 JALAPEÑO CHILE PEPPERS, STEMMED, SEEDED, AND FINELY DICED

SALT, TO TASTE

1 CUP FRESH CILANTRO, CHOPPED

Place the tomatoes, onion, and chiles in a small mixing bowl and stir to combine. Season the pico de gallo with salt, stir in the cilantro, and refrigerate the salsa for 15 minutes before serving.

SALSA MACHA

YIELD: 2 CUPS / **TOTAL TIME:** 30 MINUTES

1 CUP RAW UNSALTED PEANUTS

2 CUPS EXTRA-VIRGIN OLIVE OIL

5 GARLIC CLOVES, SLICED

1 SHALLOT, SLICED

¼ CUP SUNFLOWER SEEDS

½ TEASPOON CUMIN SEEDS

½ TEASPOON FENNEL SEEDS

1 TABLESPOON WHITE SESAME SEEDS

1 TABLESPOON BLACK SESAME SEEDS

1 TABLESPOON CORIANDER SEEDS

2 ANCHO CHILE PEPPERS, STEMMED AND SEEDED

2 GUAJILLO CHILE PEPPERS, STEMMED AND SEEDED

5 CHILES DE ÁRBOL, STEMMED AND SEEDED

1 TEASPOON APPLE CIDER VINEGAR

SALT, TO TASTE

Place the peanuts and olive oil in a medium saucepan and cook over medium-low heat, stirring occasionally, until the peanuts start to brown, 10 to 15 minutes.

Add the remaining ingredients and cook, stirring occasionally, until the garlic and shallot have browned and all of the excess moisture has evaporated. Remove the pan from heat and let the mixture cool slightly.

Strain the mixture, reserving the oil. Using a mortar and pestle, grind the solids coarsely. Stir in the oil, season the salsa with salt, and use as desired.

APPENDIX

RAITA

YIELD: 4 SERVINGS / **TOTAL TIME:** 10 MINUTES

1 CUP FULL-FAT YOGURT

½ CUP DESEEDED AND CHOPPED PERSIAN CUCUMBER

2 TEASPOONS MINCED RED ONION

2 TABLESPOONS CHOPPED FRESH CILANTRO

1 TEASPOON FRESH LEMON JUICE

Place all of the ingredients in a mixing bowl and stir to combine. Use immediately or cover the bowl and store in the refrigerator.

MUSAENGCHAE

YIELD: 6 SERVINGS / **TOTAL TIME:** 1 HOUR

3 CUPS SHREDDED DAIKON RADISH

1 TEASPOON GOCHUGARU

2 TABLESPOONS RICE VINEGAR

1 TABLESPOON KOSHER SALT

1 TABLESPOON SUGAR

Place all of the ingredients in a bowl and stir to combine.

Let the musaengchae marinate in the refrigerator for 1 hour before serving.

CORN TORTILLAS

YIELD: 32 TORTILLAS / **TOTAL TIME:** 30 MINUTES

1 LB. MASA HARINA

1½ TABLESPOONS KOSHER SALT

3 CUPS WARM FILTERED WATER, PLUS MORE AS NEEDED

In the work bowl of stand mixer fitted with the paddle attachment, combine the masa harina and salt. With the mixer on low speed, slowly begin to add the water. The mixture should come together as a soft, smooth dough. You want the masa to be moist enough so that when a small ball of it is pressed flat in your hands, the edges do not crack. Also, the masa should not stick to your hands when you peel it off your palm.

Let the masa rest for 10 minutes and check the hydration again. You may need to add more water depending on environmental conditions.

Warm a cast-iron skillet over high heat. Portion the masa into 1 oz. balls and cover them with a damp linen towel.

Line a tortilla press with two 8-inch circles of plastic. You can use a grocery store bag, a resealable bag, or even a standard kitchen trash bag as a source for the plastic. Place a masa ball in the center of one circle and gently push down on it with the palm of one hand to flatten. Place the other plastic circle on top and then close the tortilla press, applying firm, even pressure to flatten the masa into a round tortilla.

Open the tortilla press and remove the top layer of plastic. Carefully pick up the tortilla and remove the bottom piece of plastic.

Gently lay the tortilla flat in the pan, taking care to not wrinkle it. Cook for 15 to 30 seconds, until the edge begins to lift up slightly. Turn the tortilla over and let it cook for 30 to 45 seconds before turning it over one last time. If the hydration of the masa was correct and the heat is high enough, the tortilla should puff up and inflate. Remove the tortilla from the pan and store in a tortilla warmer lined with a linen towel. Repeat until all of the prepared masa has been made into tortillas.

PITA BREAD

YIELD: 8 SERVINGS / **TOTAL TIME:** 3 HOURS

1 CUP LUKEWARM WATER (90°F)

1 TABLESPOON ACTIVE DRY YEAST

1 TABLESPOON SUGAR

1¾ CUPS ALL-PURPOSE FLOUR, PLUS MORE AS NEEDED

1 CUP WHOLE WHEAT FLOUR

1 TABLESPOON KOSHER SALT

In a large mixing bowl, combine the water, yeast, and sugar. Let the mixture sit until it starts to foam, about 15 minutes.

Add the flours and salt and work the mixture until it comes together as a smooth dough. Cover the bowl with a kitchen towel and let it rise for about 15 minutes.

Preheat the oven to 500°F and place a baking stone on the floor of the oven.

Divide the dough into eight pieces and form them into balls. Place the balls on a flour-dusted work surface, press them down, and roll them until they are about ¼ inch thick.

Working with one pita at a time, place the pita on the baking stone and bake until it is puffy and brown, about 8 minutes. Remove each pita from the oven and serve warm or at room temperature.

SPICED PEPITAS

YIELD: 1 CUP / **TOTAL TIME:** 45 MINUTES

1 CUP PEPITAS

1 TABLESPOON EXTRA-VIRGIN OLIVE OIL

2 TEASPOONS ADVIEH

1 TEASPOON SALT

1 TEASPOON BLACK PEPPER

Preheat the oven to 325°F and line a baking sheet with parchment paper.

Place all of the ingredients in a bowl and toss to combine. Transfer the pepitas to the baking sheet, place them in the oven, and toast until they are golden brown, about 10 minutes.

Remove the pepitas from the oven and let them cool before using or storing in an airtight container.

COLESLAW

YIELD: 6 SERVINGS / **TOTAL TIME:** 40 MINUTES

¼ CUP APPLE CIDER VINEGAR

¼ CUP HONEY

1 GARLIC CLOVE, MINCED

1 TEASPOON CELERY SALT

1 TEASPOON BLACK PEPPER

1 TEASPOON KOSHER SALT

½ TEASPOON MUSTARD POWDER

2 CARROTS, PEELED AND SHREDDED

½ HEAD OF RED CABBAGE, CORE REMOVED, SHREDDED

½ HEAD OF GREEN CABBAGE, CORE REMOVED, SHREDDED

Place all of the ingredients, except for the carrots and cabbages, in a saucepan and bring to a boil. Reduce the heat, simmer for 5 minutes, and remove the pan from heat.

Place the cabbages and carrots in a heatproof bowl, pour the dressing over it, and stir to combine.

Refrigerate the coleslaw for 30 minutes before serving.

LEMON & PARMESAN VINAIGRETTE

YIELD: 1¼ CUPS / **TOTAL TIME:** 5 MINUTES

1 EGG YOLK

¼ CUP GRATED PARMESAN CHEESE

2 TABLESPOONS FRESH LEMON JUICE

1 TEASPOON DIJON MUSTARD

1 CUP CANOLA OIL

Place all of the ingredients, except for the canola oil, in a small bowl and stir to combine. While whisking continually, slowly stream in the canola oil until it has emulsified.

Taste, adjust the seasoning as necessary, and use as desired.

LEMON & HONEY VINAIGRETTE

YIELD: ½ CUP / **TOTAL TIME:** 5 MINUTES

ZEST AND JUICE OF 2 LEMONS

2 TEASPOONS HONEY

½ TEASPOON DIJON MUSTARD

2 TEASPOONS MINCED SHALLOT

4 LARGE FRESH BASIL LEAVES, TORN

½ TEASPOON KOSHER SALT

¼ TEASPOON BLACK PEPPER

⅓ CUP EXTRA-VIRGIN OLIVE OIL

Place all of the ingredients, except for the olive oil, in a small bowl and whisk to combine. While whisking continually, slowly stream in the olive oil until it has emulsified. Use as desired.

TAHINI & DILL CAESAR DRESSING

YIELD: 1¼ CUPS / **TOTAL TIME:** 5 MINUTES

2 TABLESPOONS TAHINI PASTE

¼ CUP GRATED PARMESAN CHEESE

1 TEASPOON BLACK PEPPER

1½ TEASPOONS KOSHER SALT

3 ANCHOVIES IN OLIVE OIL, DRAINED

ZEST OF 1 LEMON

2 TABLESPOONS FRESH LEMON JUICE

3 EGG YOLKS

1 TABLESPOON DIJON MUSTARD

¾ CUP CANOLA OIL

1 TABLESPOON CHOPPED FRESH DILL

Place all of the ingredients, except for the canola oil and dill, in a food processor and blitz to combine.

With the food processor running, slowly stream in the canola oil until it has emulsified.

Taste the dressing and adjust the seasoning as necessary. Add the dill and pulse until it has been incorporated. Use as desired.

APPLE BUTTER

YIELD: 3 CUPS / **TOTAL TIME:** 2 HOURS

3 CUPS BRANDY

5 LBS. APPLES, RINSED WELL

½ CUP PURE MAPLE SYRUP

¼ CUP BROWN SUGAR

1 TEASPOON FINE SEA SALT

½ TEASPOON CINNAMON

¼ TEASPOON CORIANDER

¼ TEASPOON GROUND CLOVES

¼ TEASPOON NUTMEG

Place the brandy in a saucepan, bring it to a boil over medium-high heat, and cook until it has reduced by half, about 15 minutes. Remove the pan from heat and set it aside.

Cut the apples into quarters, remove the cores, place them in a stockpot, and cover them with cold water. Bring to a boil over medium-high heat and then reduce the heat so that the apples simmer. Cook until tender, about 15 minutes, and then drain.

Preheat the oven to 225°F. Run the apples through a food mill and catch the pulp in a mixing bowl. Add the reduced brandy and the remaining ingredients, stir to combine, and transfer the mixture to a shallow baking dish.

Place the baking dish in the oven and bake the apple mixture, stirring every 10 minutes or so, until all of the excess water has evaporated, 1 to 1½ hours.

Remove the baking dish from the oven, transfer the mixture to a food processor, and blitz until smooth. Use immediately or store in the refrigerator.

ESCABECHE

YIELD: 4 CUPS / **TOTAL TIME:** 2 HOURS

3 JALAPEÑO CHILE PEPPERS, STEMMED, SEEDED, AND SLICED

1 CARROT, PEELED AND SLICED

½ WHITE ONION, SLICED THIN

2 GARLIC CLOVES

FLORETS FROM ½ HEAD OF CAULIFLOWER

1 TEASPOON DRIED MARJORAM

1 TEASPOON DRIED MEXICAN OREGANO

1 BAY LEAF

2 TABLESPOONS KOSHER SALT

½ TEASPOON SUGAR

1½ CUPS WHITE VINEGAR

Place the jalapeños, carrot, onion, garlic, and cauliflower in a bowl and toss to combine.

Place the marjoram, oregano, bay leaf, salt, and sugar in a bowl and stir to combine.

Place the spice mixture in a small saucepan along with the vinegar. Bring the mixture to a boil.

Pour the hot brine over the vegetables and let cool completely.

Transfer the vegetables and brine to a sterilized mason jar and store in the refrigerator for up to 1 month.

BALSAMIC GLAZE

YIELD: ½ CUP / **TOTAL TIME:** 25 MINUTES

1 CUP BALSAMIC VINEGAR

¼ CUP BROWN SUGAR

Place the vinegar and brown sugar in a small saucepan and bring the mixture to a boil.

Reduce the heat to medium-low and simmer for 8 to 10 minutes, stirring frequently, until the mixture has thickened.

Remove the pan from heat and let the glaze cool for 15 minutes before using.

GREEN GODDESS PESTO

YIELD: 1½ CUPS / **TOTAL TIME:** 10 MINUTES

¼ CUP CHOPPED CELERY LEAVES

½ CUP CHOPPED FRESH PARSLEY

2 TABLESPOONS CHOPPED FRESH TARRAGON

½ CUP SLICED FRESH CHIVES

¾ CUP SUNFLOWER SEEDS, TOASTED

2 TEASPOONS FINE SEA SALT

1 TEASPOON BLACK PEPPER

1 TEASPOON FRESH LEMON JUICE

ZEST OF 1 LEMON

¾ CUP CANOLA OIL

¼ CUP EXTRA-VIRGIN OLIVE OIL

Place all of the ingredients, except for the oils, in a food processor and blitz to combine.

With the food processor running, slowly stream in the oils until they have emulsified.

Taste the pesto, adjust the seasoning as necessary, and either use immediately or store in the refrigerator.

PICKLED RED ONION

YIELD: 2 CUPS / **TOTAL TIME:** 2 HOURS

1 LARGE RED ONION, SLICED

2 CUPS RED WINE VINEGAR

1 TEASPOON FENNEL SEEDS

1 TEASPOON MUSTARD SEEDS

½ TEASPOON CELERY SEEDS

⅓ CUP SUGAR

1 TEASPOON KOSHER SALT

Place the onion in a mason jar. Place the remaining ingredients in a small saucepan and bring to a boil, stirring to dissolve the sugar and salt.

Pour the brine over the onion, making sure it is completely submerged, and let it cool completely before serving or storing in the refrigerator.

LICENSE TO GRILL

SPICY MAYONNAISE

YIELD: 1¼ CUPS / **TOTAL TIME:** 5 MINUTES

1 TABLESPOON EPIS (SEE PAGE 193)

1 CUP MAYONNAISE

2 TABLESPOONS KETCHUP

1 TABLESPOON SLICED SCALLION

1 TEASPOON ADOBO SEASONING

1 TEASPOON GARLIC POWDER

½ TEASPOON SAZÓN

½ TEASPOON PAPRIKA

¼ TEASPOON CAYENNE PEPPER

Place all of the ingredients in a bowl and stir until well combined. Use immediately or store in the refrigerator.

CHICKEN STOCK

YIELD: 8 CUPS / **TOTAL TIME:** 6 HOURS

7 LBS. CHICKEN BONES, RINSED

4 CUPS CHOPPED YELLOW ONIONS

2 CUPS CHOPPED CARROTS

2 CUPS CHOPPED CELERY

3 GARLIC CLOVES, CRUSHED

3 SPRIGS OF FRESH THYME

1 TEASPOON BLACK PEPPERCORNS

1 BAY LEAF

Place the chicken bones in a stockpot and cover them with cold water. Bring to a simmer over medium-high heat and use a ladle to skim off any impurities that rise to the surface.

Add the vegetables, thyme, peppercorns, and bay leaf, reduce the heat to low, and simmer for 5 hours, skimming the stock occasionally to remove any impurities that rise to the surface.

Strain the stock, let it cool slightly, and transfer it to the refrigerator. Leave the stock uncovered and let it cool completely. Remove the layer of fat and cover. The stock will keep in the refrigerator for 3 to 5 days, and in the freezer for up to 3 months.

TARE SAUCE

YIELD: 2 CUPS / **TOTAL TIME:** 30 MINUTES

½ CUP CHICKEN STOCK (SEE PAGE 215)

½ CUP SOY SAUCE

½ CUP MIRIN

¼ CUP SAKE

½ CUP BROWN SUGAR

2 GARLIC CLOVES, SMASHED

1 TABLESPOON MINCED GINGER

2 SCALLIONS, TRIMMED AND SLICED

Place all of the ingredients in a small saucepan and bring to a simmer over low heat. Simmer for 10 minutes, stirring once or twice.

Remove the pan from heat and let the sauce cool completely. Strain before using or storing.

CLARIFIED BUTTER

YIELD: ¾ CUP / **TOTAL TIME:** 10 MINUTES

1 CUP UNSALTED BUTTER

Place the butter in a saucepan and melt it over medium heat.

Reduce the heat to the lowest possible setting. Cook until the butter fat is very clear and the milk solids drop to the bottom of the pan.

Skim the foam from the surface of the butter and discard it. Strain the butter into a container and use as desired.

FENNEL PESTO

YIELD: 2½ CUPS / **TOTAL TIME:** 15 MINUTES

¾ CUP PINE NUTS

1 CUP CHOPPED FENNEL FRONDS

½ CUP FRESH PARSLEY

10 FRESH MINT LEAVES

1 TEASPOON FINE SEA SALT

½ TEASPOON BLACK PEPPER

1 TEASPOON FRESH LEMON JUICE

ZEST OF 1 LEMON

¼ CUP CANOLA OIL

1 TABLESPOON EXTRA-VIRGIN OLIVE OIL

Preheat the oven to 350°F. Place the pine nuts on a baking sheet and place them in the oven. Toast the pine nuts until they are fragrant and browned, about 6 minutes. Remove the pine nuts from the oven and set them aside.

Place the toasted pine nuts and all of the remaining ingredients, except for the oils, in a food processor and blitz to combine. With the food processor running, slowly stream in the oils until they have emulsified.

Taste the pesto, adjust the seasoning as necessary, and use immediately or store in the refrigerator.

CONVERSION TABLE

Weights

1 oz. = 28 grams
2 oz. = 57 grams
4 oz. (¼ lb.) = 113 grams
8 oz. (½ lb.) = 227 grams
16 oz. (1 lb.) = 454 grams

Volume Measures

⅛ teaspoon = 0.6 ml
¼ teaspoon = 1.23 ml
½ teaspoon = 2.5 ml
1 teaspoon = 5 ml
1 tablespoon (3 teaspoons) = ½ fluid oz. = 15 ml
2 tablespoons = 1 fluid oz. = 29.5 ml
¼ cup (4 tablespoons) = 2 fluid oz. = 59 ml
⅓ cup (5⅓ tablespoons) = 2.7 fluid oz. = 80 ml
½ cup (8 tablespoons) = 4 fluid oz. = 120 ml
⅔ cup (10⅔ tablespoons) = 5.4 fluid oz. = 160 ml
¾ cup (12 tablespoons) = 6 fluid oz. = 180 ml
1 cup (16 tablespoons) = 8 fluid oz. = 240 ml

Temperature Equivalents

°F	°C	Gas Mark
225	110	¼
250	130	½
275	140	1
300	150	2
325	170	3
350	180	4
375	190	5
400	200	6
425	220	7
450	230	8
475	240	9
500	250	10

Length Measures

1/16 inch = 1.6 mm
⅛ inch = 3 mm
¼ inch = 6.35 mm
½ inch = 1.25 cm
¾ inch = 2 cm
1 inch = 2.5 cm

INDEX

A

Acapulco Gold Rub, 174
achiote paste
    Recado Rojo, 193
adobo seasoning
    Creole Smash Burgers, 31
    Jerk Spice Rub, 186
    Spicy Mayonnaise, 215
almonds
    Romesco Sauce, 198
American cheese
    Bacon Cheeseburger, 40
anchovies
    Tahini & Dill Caesar Dressing, 211
andouille sausage
    Shrimp Boil, 100
Apple Butter
    Poached & Grilled Delicata Squash, 155
    recipe, 212
apples
    Apple Butter, 212
    Grilled Romaine & Crispy Sweet Potato, 167
    Mole Manchamanteles, 191
    Poached & Grilled Delicata Squash, 155
Asparagus, Grilled, 165
avocados
    Sweet Corn & Pepita Guacamole, 127

B

Baby Bok Choy with Salsa Macha, 146
bacon
    Bacon Cheeseburger, 40
    BBQ Burgers, 43
    Creole Smash Burgers, 31
bacon fat
    Brown Sugar Ribs, 73
Balsamic Glaze
    Cantaloupe & Mozzarella with Balsamic Glaze, 124
    recipe, 213
basil
    Summer Squash Salad, 158

Bay Blend Marinade, 189
BBQ Brisket, 35
BBQ Burgers, 43
BBQ Poultry Rub, 186
BBQ Sauce
    BBQ Burgers, 43
    Brown Sugar Ribs, 73
    Coffee & Bourbon BBQ Sauce, 201
    Kansas City BBQ Sauce, 200
    Molasses BBQ Sauce, 201
    Smoky Southern BBQ Sauce, 199
    South Carolina BBQ Sauce, 200
BBQ Shrimp, New Orleans Style, 111
beef
    Bacon Cheeseburger, 40
    BBQ Brisket, 35
    BBQ Burgers, 43
    Beef Kebabs, 44
    Beef Shawarma, 48
    Carne Asada, 47
    Chile-Rubbed London Broil, 30
    Chipotle T-Bone, 18
    Coffee-Rubbed Sirloin, 24
    Creole Smash Burgers, 31
    Filet Mignon, 27
    Flank Steak, 23
    New York Strip, 15
    Porterhouse, 19
    Prime Rib, 37
    Red Wine & Herb Tri-Tip Steak, 36
    Rib Eye, 16
    Strip Steaks with Peppercorn Cream Sauce, 28
Beets with Dukkah, Grilled, 149
Blackened Salmon, 94
Blackening Spice
    Blackened Salmon, 94
    recipe, 182
Bok Choy with Salsa Macha, Baby, 146
brandy
    Apple Butter, 212
Branzino, Whole, 103

Brisket, BBQ, 35
Brisket Rub, 176
Broccoli with Lemon & Parmesan Vinaigrette, Charred, 135
Brown Sugar Ribs, 73
Buffalo Wings, 145

C

cabbage
    Coleslaw, 210
    Grilled Cabbage, 154
Cajun Rub, 183
Cajun Tilapia, 102
Cantaloupe & Mozzarella with Balsamic Glaze, 124
Caramelized Plums with Fennel, Orange, Ginger Yogurt & Pine Nuts, 151
Carne Asada, 47
carrots
    Chicken Stock, 215
    Coleslaw, 210
    Escabeche, 213
cauliflower
    Escabeche, 213
Cecina de Cerdo, 63
Cedar-Plank Salmon, 115
celery
    Bay Blend Marinade, 189
    Chicken Stock, 215
    Salmon & Vegetable Skewers, 114
celery leaves
    Green Goddess Pesto, 214
Charred Broccoli with Lemon & Parmesan Vinaigrette, 135
Charred Eggplant, 162
cheddar cheese
    BBQ Burgers, 43
    Creole Smash Burgers, 31
cheese. *See individual cheese types*
Chermoula Sea Bass, 119
chicken
    Buffalo Wings, 145

Chicken Kebabs, 67
Chicken Souvlaki, 77
Chicken Teriyaki Burgers, 76
Chicken Tsukune, 170
Jamaican Jerk Chicken, 58
Jerk Chicken Wings, 131
Peri-Peri Chicken, 57
Rotisserie Chicken, 81
Smoky & Spicy Chicken Wings, 144
Za'atar Chicken, 83
Chicken Stock
    Chorizo-Stuffed Mushrooms, 169
    Mole Manchamanteles, 191
    Octopus al Pastor, 108–109
    recipe, 215
    Tare Sauce, 216
Chile Rub, 180
Chile-Rubbed London Broil, 30
Chiles Rellenos, 130
Chimichurri Sauce
    Grilled Lamb Loin with Chimichurri, 51
    recipe, 196
    Red Wine & Herb Tri-Tip Steak, 36
Chipotle T-Bone, 18
chives
    Green Goddess Pesto, 214
    Red Chermoula Sauce, 196
Chorizo-Stuffed Mushrooms, 169
cilantro
    Carne Asada, 47
    Elotes, 152
    leysters, 159
    Lobster Mojo de Ajo, 107
    Peri-Peri Marinade, 190
    Pico de Gallo, 205
    Pork Toro with Salsa Macha, 59
    Raita, 207
    Red Chermoula Sauce, 196
    Sweet Corn & Pepita Guacamole, 127
Citrus & Sage Marinade, 189
Clarified Butter
    Buffalo Wings, 145
    recipe, 216
coffee
    Coffee & Bourbon BBQ Sauce, 201
    Coffee-Rubbed Sirloin, 24
Cognac
    Strip Steaks with Peppercorn Cream Sauce, 28
Coleslaw
    BBQ Brisket, 35
    recipe, 210
conversion tables, 218
corn
    Elotes, 152
    Sweet Corn & Pepita Guacamole, 127
Corn Tortillas
    Cecina de Cerdo, 63
    Grilled Quail, 74
    Lomo y Manchamanteles, 62

Octopus al Pastor, 108–109
Pescado Zarandeado, 95
    recipe, 208
Cream Sauce, Strip Steaks with Peppercorn, 28
Creole Smash Burgers, 31
cucumbers
    Beef Shawarma, 48
    Raita, 207

D
daikon radish
    Musaengchae, 207
Delicata Squash, Poached & Grilled, 155
Dill Caesar Dressing, Tahini &
    Radicchio with Tahini & Dill Caesar Dressing, 143
    recipe, 211
Dukkah, Grilled Beets with, 149
Dwaeji Bulgogi, 90

E
Eggplant, Charred, 162
eggs/egg whites
    Bacon Cheeseburger, 40
    BBQ Burgers, 43
    Chicken Tsukune, 170
    Chiles Rellenos, 130
    Tahini & Dill Caesar Dressing, 211
Elotes, 152
epazote
    Octopus al Pastor, 108–109
Epis
    Creole Smash Burgers, 31
    Jerk Spice Rub, 186
    recipe, 193
    Spicy Mayonnaise, 215
Escabeche
    Pavo en Escabeche, 66
    recipe, 213

F
fennel
    Caramelized Plums with Fennel, Orange, Ginger
      Yogurt & Pine Nuts, 151
    Fennel Pesto, 217
    Tuna with Orange & Fennel Salad, 118
feta cheese
    Grilled Romaine & Crispy Sweet Potato, 167
    Summer Squash Salad, 158
Fig & Goat Cheese Salad, 125
Filet Mignon, 27
Fire-Roasted Peppers & Onions, 163
fish
    Blackened Salmon, 94
    Cajun Tilapia, 102
    Cedar-Plank Salmon, 115
    Chermoula Sea Bass, 119
    Grilled Sardines with Lemon & Herbs, 139
    Honey & Soy-Glazed Rainbow Trout, 110
    Pescado Zarandeado, 95

Salmon & Vegetable Skewers, 114
Swordfish, 121
Tuna with Orange & Fennel Salad, 118
Whole Branzino, 103
See also seafood
Five-Alarm Rub, 181
flank steaks
    Carne Asada, 47
    Flank Steak, 23

G
garlic
    Bay Blend Marinade, 189
    Beef Kebabs, 44
    Buffalo Wings, 145
    Carne Asada, 47
    Cecina de Cerdo, 63
    Chicken Souvlaki, 77
    Chicken Stock, 215
    Chiles Rellenos, 130
    Chimichurri Sauce, 196
    Citrus & Sage Marinade, 189
    Coleslaw, 210
    Dwaeji Bulgogi, 90
    Epis, 193
    Escabeche, 213
    Grilled Sardines with Lemon & Herbs, 139
    Kansas City BBQ Sauce, 200
    Lamb Kebabs, 52
    Lamb Marinade, 188
    Lobster Mojo de Ajo, 107
    Molasses BBQ Sauce, 201
    Mole Manchamanteles, 191
    Mussels in White Wine & Herbs, 99
    Octopus al Pastor, 108–109
    Pavo en Escabeche, 66
    Peri-Peri Marinade, 190
    Pescado Zarandeado, 95
    Poached & Grilled Delicata Squash, 155
    Poultry Brine, 187
    Prime Rib, 37
    Recado Rojo, 193
    Red Wine & Herb Marinade, 188
    Romesco Sauce, 198
    Rosemary & Lemon Leg of Lamb, 50
    Rustic Steak Rub, 176
    Salmon & Vegetable Skewers, 114
    Salsa Macha, 205
    Shrimp Boil, 100
    Smoky & Spicy Chicken Wings, 144
    Smoky Southern BBQ Sauce, 199
    South Carolina BBQ Sauce, 200
    Spicy Southwestern Rub, 182
    Tare Sauce, 216
    Vegetable Kebabs, 148
ginger, fresh
    Caramelized Plums with Fennel, Orange, Ginger
      Yogurt & Pine Nuts, 151
    Dwaeji Bulgogi, 90

LICENSE TO GRILL

220

Smoky Southern BBQ Sauce, 199
Tare Sauce, 216
goat cheese
Elotes, 152
Fig & Goat Cheese Salad, 125
Grilled Goat Cheese, 138
gochugaru
Musaengchae, 207
gochujang
Dwaeji Bulgogi, 90
grapefruit juice
Octopus al Pastor, 108–109
Recado Rojo, 193
Green Goddess Pesto
Grilled Pork Loin with Green Goddess Pesto, 88
recipe, 214
Grilled Asparagus, 165
Grilled Beets with Dukkah, 149
Grilled Cabbage, 154
Grilled Goat Cheese, 138
Grilled Lamb Loin with Chimichurri, 51
Grilled Leeks with Romesco, 166
Grilled Oysters, 159
Grilled Pork Loin with Green Goddess Pesto, 88
Grilled Quail, 74
Grilled Romaine & Crispy Sweet Potato, 167
Grilled Sardines with Lemon & Herbs, 139

H

Harissa
Red Chermoula Sauce, 196
hazelnuts
Grilled Beets with Dukkah, 149
honey
Cedar-Plank Salmon, 115
Coleslaw, 210
Honey & Soy-Glazed Rainbow Trout, 110
Lomo y Manchamanteles, 62
Molasses BBQ Sauce, 201
Peach Salad with Lemon & Honey Vinaigrette, 136
Peri-Peri Marinade, 190
Sesame & Honey Marinade, 190
South Carolina BBQ Sauce, 200
Vegetable Kebabs, 148
hot sauce
Buffalo Wings, 145
Jerk Chicken Wings, 131
Remoulade Sauce, 198
Spicy Turkey Wings, 168

J

Jamaican Jerk Chicken, 58
Jerk Chicken Wings, 131
Jerk Marinade
Jamaican Jerk Chicken, 58
recipe, 187
Jerk Spice Rub
Jerk Chicken Wings, 131
recipe, 186

K

Kansas City BBQ Sauce, 200
Kashmiri Chile Rub
recipe, 180
Spicy Lamb Chops with Raita, 49
kecap manis
Sesame & Honey Marinade, 190

L

lamb
Grilled Lamb Loin with Chimichurri, 51
Lamb Kebabs, 52
Rosemary & Lemon Leg of Lamb, 50
Spicy Lamb Chops with Raita, 49
Lamb Marinade
Grilled Lamb Loin with Chimichurri, 51
recipe, 188
Leeks with Romesco, Grilled, 166
Lemon & Herb Poultry Rub, 175
Lemon & Honey Vinaigrette
Peach Salad with, 136
recipe, 211
Lemon & Parmesan Vinaigrette
Charred Broccoli with, 135
recipe, 210
lemons/lemon juice
Beef Shawarma, 48
Lemon & Parmesan Vinaigrette, 211
Remoulade Sauce, 198
Rosemary & Lemon Leg of Lamb, 50
Shrimp Boil, 100
limes
Honey & Soy-Glazed Rainbow Trout, 110
limes/lime juice
Elotes, 152
Epis, 193
Grilled Oysters, 159
Peri-Peri Marinade, 190
Pescado Zarandeado, 95
Recado Rojo, 193
Smoky & Spicy Chicken Wings, 144
Lobster Mojo de Ajo, 107
Lomo y Manchamanteles, 62
London Broil, Chile-Rubbed, 30

M

maple syrup
Apple Butter, 212
Cedar-Plank Salmon, 115
mesclun greens
Tuna with Orange & Fennel Salad, 118
mint
Beef Shawarma, 48
Fennel Pesto, 217
mirin
Chicken Tsukune, 170
Tare Sauce, 216
molasses
Coffee & Bourbon BBQ Sauce, 201

Kansas City BBQ Sauce, 200
Molasses BBQ Sauce, 201
Slow-Cooked Molasses BBQ Ribs, 70
Mole Manchamanteles
Lomo y Manchamanteles, 62
recipe, 191
Mole Rub, 175
Monterey Jack cheese
Chiles Rellenos, 130
mozzarella cheese
Cantaloupe & Mozzarella with Balsamic Glaze, 124
Peach Salad with Lemon & Honey Vinaigrette, 136
Musaengchae
Dwaeji Bulgogi, 90
recipe, 207
mushrooms
Baby Bok Choy with Salsa Macha, 146
Chorizo-Stuffed Mushrooms, 169
Vegetable Kebabs, 148
Mussels in White Wine & Herbs, 99

N

New York Strip, 15
nuts. *See individual nut types*

O

Oaxaca cheese
Chiles Rellenos, 130
Octopus al Pastor, 108–109
olives
Grilled Goat Cheese, 138
onion
Baby Bok Choy with Salsa Macha, 146
Bay Blend Marinade, 189
Beef Kebabs, 44
Beef Shawarma, 48
Charred Eggplant, 162
Chicken Stock, 215
Chiles Rellenos, 130
Chorizo-Stuffed Mushrooms, 169
Creole Smash Burgers, 31
Epis, 193
Escabeche, 213
Fire-Roasted Peppers & Onions, 163
Jerk Marinade, 187
Lamb Kebabs, 52
Mole Manchamanteles, 191
Octopus al Pastor, 108–109
Pickled Red Onion, 214
Pico de Gallo, 205
Raita, 207
Red Wine & Herb Marinade, 188
Smoky Southern BBQ Sauce, 199
Sweet Corn & Pepita Guacamole, 127
Tuna with Orange & Fennel Salad, 118
orange juice
Caramelized Plums with Fennel, Orange, Ginger Yogurt & Pine Nuts, 151
Carne Asada, 47

Recado Rojo, 193
Spicy Orange Pork, 91
Tuna with Orange & Fennel Salad, 118
oranges
Caramelized Plums with Fennel, Orange, Ginger
Yogurt & Pine Nuts, 151
Citrus & Sage Marinade, 189
Fig & Goat Cheese Salad, 125
Tuna with Orange & Fennel Salad, 118

P

Parmesan cheese
Charred Broccoli with Lemon & Parmesan Vinaigrette, 135
Chorizo-Stuffed Mushrooms, 169
Lemon & Parmesan Vinaigrette, 210
Radicchio with Tahini & Dill Caesar Dressing, 143
Tahini & Dill Caesar Dressing, 211
parsley
Beef Shawarma, 48
Chimichurri Sauce, 196
Chorizo-Stuffed Mushrooms, 169
Epis, 193
Fennel Pesto, 217
Green Goddess Pesto, 214
Mussels in White Wine & Herbs, 99
Red Chermoula Sauce, 196
Romesco Sauce, 198
Salmon & Vegetable Skewers, 114
Strip Steaks with Peppercorn Cream Sauce, 28
Pavo en Escabeche, 66
peaches
Lomo y Manchamanteles, 62
Mole Manchamanteles, 191
Peach Salad with Lemon & Honey Vinaigrette, 136
peanuts
Salsa Macha, 205
pears
Mole Manchamanteles, 191
pepitas/pumpkin seeds
Poached & Grilled Delicata Squash, 155
recipe, 209
Sweet Corn & Pepita Guacamole, 127
Peppercorn Cream Sauce, Strip Steaks with, 28
peppers, bell
Baby Bok Choy with Salsa Macha, 146
Charred Eggplant, 162
Creole Smash Burgers, 31
Epis, 193
Fire-Roasted Peppers & Onions, 163
Romesco Sauce, 198
Salmon & Vegetable Skewers, 114
Vegetable Kebabs, 148
peppers, chile
BBQ Burgers, 43
Brown Sugar Ribs, 73
Carne Asada, 47
Cecina de Cerdo, 63

Chiles Rellenos, 130
Elotes, 152
Epis, 193
Escabeche, 213
Five-Alarm Rub, 181
Jerk Marinade, 187
Mole Manchamanteles, 191
Octopus al Pastor, 108–109
Pavo en Escabeche, 66
Peri-Peri Marinade, 190
Pescado Zarandeado, 95
Pickled Grilled Pineapple, 126
Pico de Gallo, 205
Pork Toro with Salsa Macha, 59
Recado Rojo, 193
Salsa Macha, 205
Smoky Southern BBQ Sauce, 199
Spicy Southwestern Rub, 182
Peri-Peri Chicken, 57
Peri-Peri Marinade, 190
Pescado Zarandeado, 95
Pickled Grilled Pineapple
Jamaican Jerk Chicken, 58
recipe, 126
pickled jalapeños
BBQ Burgers, 43
Pickled Red Onion
Charred Broccoli with Lemon & Parmesan Vinaigrette, 135
recipe, 214
Pico de Gallo, 205
piloncillo
Mole Manchamanteles, 191
pine nuts
Caramelized Plums with Fennel, Orange, Ginger
Yogurt & Pine Nuts, 151
Charred Broccoli with Lemon & Parmesan Vinaigrette, 135
Fennel Pesto, 217
pineapple
Chicken Teriyaki Burgers, 76
Pickled Grilled Pineapple, 126
pineapple juice
Octopus al Pastor, 108–109
pistachios
Grilled Beets with Dukkah, 149
Peach Salad with Lemon & Honey Vinaigrette, 136
Pita Bread
Beef Shawarma, 48
Chicken Souvlaki, 77
recipe, 209
plantains
Mole Manchamanteles, 191
Plums with Fennel, Orange, Ginger Yogurt & Pine Nuts,
Caramelized, 151
Poached & Grilled Delicata Squash, 155
pomegranate seeds
Sweet Corn & Pepita Guacamole, 127

Porchetta, 84
pork
Brown Sugar Ribs, 73
Cecina de Cerdo, 63
Dwaeji Bulgogi, 90
Grilled Pork Loin with Green Goddess Pesto, 88
Lomo y Manchamanteles, 62
Porchetta, 84
Pork Toro with Salsa Macha, 59
Slow-Cooked Molasses BBQ Ribs, 70
Spicy Orange Pork, 91
Pork Chops, 85
Porterhouse, 19
potatoes
Shrimp Boil, 100
Poultry Brine
recipe, 187
Rotisserie Chicken, 81
Prime Rib, 37
pumpkin seeds/pepitas
Poached & Grilled Delicata Squash, 155
recipe, 209
Sweet Corn & Pepita Guacamole, 127

Q

Quail, Grilled, 74

R

Radicchio with Tahini & Dill Caesar Dressing, 143
raisins
Mole Manchamanteles, 191
Raita
recipe, 207
Spicy Lamb Chops with Raita, 49
Recado Rojo
Octopus al Pastor, 108–109
recipe, 193
Red Chermoula Sauce
Chermoula Sea Bass, 119
recipe, 196
red snapper
Pescado Zarandeado, 95
Red Wine & Herb Marinade
recipe, 188
Red Wine & Herb Tri-Tip Steak, 36
Remoulade Sauce
recipe, 198
Shrimp Boil, 100
Rib Eye, 16
rice
Dwaeji Bulgogi, 90
Romaine & Crispy Sweet Potato, Grilled, 167
Romesco Sauce
Grilled Leeks with Romesco, 166
recipe, 198
rosemary
Flank Steak, 23
Porchetta, 84

Prime Rib, 37
Red Wine & Herb Marinade, 188
Rosemary & Lemon Leg of Lamb, 50
Rotisserie Chicken, 81
Rustic Steak Rub, 176

S

saffron
Red Chermoula Sauce, 196
sage
Citrus & Sage Marinade, 189
Poached & Grilled Delicata Squash, 155
Porchetta, 84
sake
Chicken Tsukune, 170
Tare Sauce, 216
salmon
Blackened Salmon, 94
Cedar-Plank Salmon, 115
Salmon & Vegetable Skewers, 114
Salsa Macha
Baby Bok Choy with Salsa Macha, 146
Pork Toro with Salsa Macha, 59
recipe, 205
Sardines with Lemon & Herbs, Grilled, 139
sausage
Chorizo-Stuffed Mushrooms, 169
Shrimp Boil, 100
scallions
Dwaeji Bulgogi, 90
Epis, 193
Jerk Marinade, 187
Spicy Mayonnaise, 215
Tare Sauce, 216
Sea Bass, Chermoula, 119
seafood
BBQ Shrimp, New Orleans Style, 111
Grilled Oysters, 159
Lobster Mojo de Ajo, 107
Mussels in White Wine & Herbs, 99
Octopus al Pastor, 108–109
Shrimp Boil, 100
See also fish
Seafood Rub
recipe, 177
Swordfish, 121
Sesame & Honey Marinade, 190
sesame seeds
Mole Manchamanteles, 191
Salsa Macha, 205
shallots
Grilled Sardines with Lemon & Herbs, 139
Lemon & Parmesan Vinaigrette, 211
Mussels in White Wine & Herbs, 99
Prime Rib, 37
Salsa Macha, 205
Strip Steaks with Peppercorn Cream Sauce, 28

shrimp
BBQ Shrimp, New Orleans Style, 111
Shrimp Boil, 100
sirloin
Beef Shawarma, 48
Coffee-Rubbed Sirloin, 24
Slow-Cooked Molasses BBQ Ribs, 70
Smoked Paprika Rub, 177
Smoky & Spicy Chicken Wings, 144
Smoky Southern BBQ Sauce, 199
Smoky St. Louis Rub, 181
South Carolina BBQ Sauce, 200
soy sauce
Honey & Soy-Glazed Rainbow Trout, 110
Pork Toro with Salsa Macha, 59
Tare Sauce, 216
Tuna with Orange & Fennel Salad, 118
Spatchcock Turkey, 80
Spiced Pepitas
Poached & Grilled Delicata Squash, 155
recipe, 209
Spicy Lamb Chops with Raita, 49
Spicy Mayonnaise
Creole Smash Burgers, 31
recipe, 215
Spicy Orange Pork, 91
Spicy Southwestern Rub, 182
Spicy Turkey Wings, 168
spinach
Summer Squash Salad, 158
squash, winter
Poached & Grilled Delicata Squash, 155
Squash Salad, Summer, 158
sriracha
Remoulade Sauce, 198
Strip Steaks with Peppercorn Cream Sauce, 28
Summer Squash Salad, 158
sunflower seeds
Green Goddess Pesto, 214
Salsa Macha, 205
Sweet & Spicy Rub, 174
Sweet Corn & Pepita Guacamole, 127
Sweet Potato, Grilled Romaine & Crispy, 167
Swordfish, 121

T

Tahini & Dill Caesar Dressing
Radicchio with Tahini & Dill Caesar Dressing, 143
recipe, 211
Tare Sauce
Chicken Tsukune, 170
recipe, 216
T-Bone, Chipotle, 18
thyme
Flank Steak, 23
Poached & Grilled Delicata Squash, 155
Porchetta, 84

Prime Rib, 37
Red Wine & Herb Marinade, 188
Tilapia, Cajun, 102
tomatoes
Beef Shawarma, 48
Chiles Rellenos, 130
Chorizo-Stuffed Mushrooms, 169
Mole Manchamanteles, 191
Peach Salad with Lemon & Honey Vinaigrette, 136
Pico de Gallo, 205
Romesco Sauce, 198
Salmon & Vegetable Skewers, 114
Smoky Southern BBQ Sauce, 199
Summer Squash Salad, 158
Trout, Honey & Soy-Glazed Rainbow, 110
Tuna with Orange & Fennel Salad, 118
turkey
Pavo en Escabeche, 66
Spatchcock Turkey, 80
Spicy Turkey Wings, 168

V

Vegetable Kebabs, 148

W

walnuts
Grilled Beets with Dukkah, 149
Grilled Goat Cheese, 138
Whole Branzino, 103
wine, red
Fig & Goat Cheese Salad, 125
Red Wine & Herb Marinade, 188
Red Wine & Herb Tri-Tip Steak, 36
wine, white
Chicken Souvlaki, 77
Mussels in White Wine & Herbs, 99

Y

yogurt
Beef Shawarma, 48
Caramelized Plums with Fennel, Orange, Ginger Yogurt & Pine Nuts, 151
Chicken Kebabs, 67
Grilled Beets with Dukkah, 149
Lamb Kebabs, 52
Raita, 207

Z

Za'atar
recipe, 183
Za'atar Chicken, 83
zucchini
Summer Squash Salad, 158
Vegetable Kebabs, 148

ABOUT CIDER MILL PRESS BOOK PUBLISHERS

Good ideas ripen with time. From seed to harvest, Cider Mill Press brings fine reading, information, and entertainment together between the covers of its creatively crafted books. Our Cider Mill bears fruit twice a year, publishing a new crop of titles each spring and fall.

"Where Good Books Are Ready for Press"

501 Nelson Place
Nashville, Tennessee 37214

cidermillpress.com